LIFE PICTURE PUZZLE

WELCOME TO LIFE'S FOURTH
PICTURE
PUZZLE
BOOK

It's amazing: When we published our first Picture Puzzle book, we never expected the response would be so overwhelming that we'd have to immediately go back to the laboratory to create another book. After the second one came out, we thought it might satisfy you, but we were wrong. The letters and e-mails came pouring in, asking for—no, demanding—more puzzles. With our first and second books simultaneously No. 1 and No. 2 on *The New York Times* best-seller list, we once again returned to this labor of love and came up with our third Picture Puzzle book.

But was that enough for you? Of course not. Those urgent phone calls and letters kept coming in, so we spent the summer carefully crafting this, our fourth Picture Puzzle book. It's much like our third book but just a bit harder for the experienced puzzle masters out there. It also contains our Guinness World Record puzzle, the biggest, baddest Picture Puzzle ever. (Dear first-time readers, welcome and don't worry—we start off gently and give you time to find your puzzle legs.)

By now we've learned our lesson: The fifth and sixth LIFE Picture Puzzle books are already in the works. Don't tell anyone, but all the photos in our next book will center on a vacation theme, featuring lots of spring, summer, fall, winter, and family fun. If you can't wait until it hits store shelves, check out our online archive of puzzles at *www.LIFE.com*. To write to us about our books, drop us a line at picturepuzzle@life.com. We'd love to hear from you.

[OUR CUT-UP PUZZLES: EASY AS 1-2-3]

We snipped a photo into 4, 6, 12, or 16 pieces. Then we rearranged the pieces and numbered them.

Your mission: Beneath each cut-up puzzle, write the number of the piece in the box where it belongs.

Check the answer key at the back of the book to see what the reassembled image looks like.

Biggest Picture Puzzle Ever! Don't forget to check out the most intense Picture Puzzle we've ever attempted on page 174. It has the greatest number of changes—80 in all—that have ever been loaded into a puzzle of its kind. And our friends at Guinness agree. How do we know? They officially named it the Largest Spot the Difference Puzzle in the world.

[HOW TO PLAY THE PUZZLES]

Dancing Fools

You'll have to step lively to keep up with our footwork here

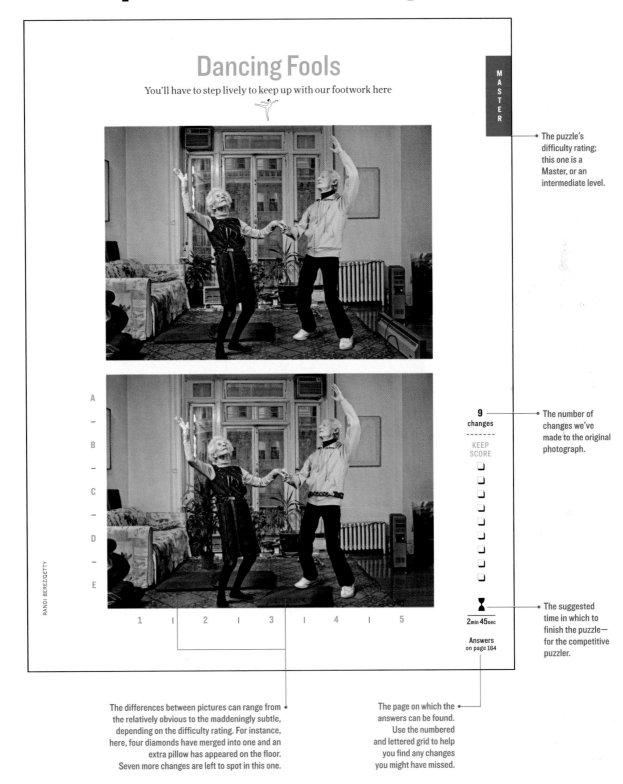

RANDI BEREZ/GETTY

MASTER

The puzzle's difficulty rating; this one is a Master, or an intermediate level.

9 changes

- - - - - - - -

KEEP SCORE

The number of changes we've made to the original photograph.

2min 45sec

Answers on page 164

The suggested time in which to finish the puzzle—for the competitive puzzler.

The differences between pictures can range from the relatively obvious to the maddeningly subtle, depending on the difficulty rating. For instance, here, four diamonds have merged into one and an extra pillow has appeared on the floor. Seven more changes are left to spot in this one.

The page on which the answers can be found. Use the numbered and lettered grid to help you find any changes you might have missed.

LIFE PICTURE PUZZLE

Puzzle Master Michael Roseman
Editor Robert Sullivan
Deputy Editor Danielle Dowling
Picture Editor Caroline Smith
Research Editor Danny Freedman
Copy Barbara Gogan
Staff Photographer Ryan Mesina

LIFE Puzzle Books
Managing Editor Bill Shapiro
Creative Director Richard Baker

LIFE Books
President Andrew Blau
Business Manager Roger Adler
Business Development Manager Jeff Burak
Business Analyst Ka-On Lee

Director of Photography Barbara Baker Burrows
Deputy Picture Editor Christina Lieberman

Editorial Operations
Richard K. Prue, David Sloan (DIRECTORS), Richard Shaffer (GROUP MANAGER),
Burt Carnesi, Brian Fellows, Raphael Joa, Angel Mass, Stanley E. Moyse (MANAGERS),
Soheila Asayesh, Keith Aurelio, Trang Ba Chuong, Ellen Bohan, Charlotte Coco,
Osmar Escalona, Kevin Hart, Norma Jones, Mert Kerimoglu, Rosalie Khan, Marco Lau,
Po Fung Ng, Rudi Papiri, Barry Pribula, Carina A. Rosario, Albert Rufino, Christopher Scala,
Diana Suryakusuma, Vaune Trachtman, Paul Tupay, Lionel Vargas, David Weiner

Time Inc. Home Entertainment
Publisher Richard Fraiman
General Manager Steven Sandonato
Executive Director, Marketing Services Carol Pittard
Director, Retail & Special Sales Tom Mifsud
Director, New Product Development Peter Harper
Assistant Director, Brand Marketing Laura Adam
Assistant General Counsel Robin Bierstedt
Book Production Manager Jonathan Polsky
Manager, Prepress & Design Anne-Michelle Gallero
Marketing Manager Alexandra Bliss

Special thanks to Bozena Bannett, Glenn Buonocore, Suzanne Janso, Robert Marasco,
Brooke Reger, Mary Sarro-Waite, Ilene Schreider, Adriana Tierno, Alex Voznesenskiy

PUBLISHED BY

LIFE BOOKS

Vol. 7, No. 6 • November 5, 2007

If you would like to order any of our hardcover Collector's Edition books, please call us at 800-327-6388
(Monday through Friday, 7 a.m. to 8 p.m., or Saturday, 7 a.m. to 6 p.m. Central Time).

READY, SET, GO!

NOVI

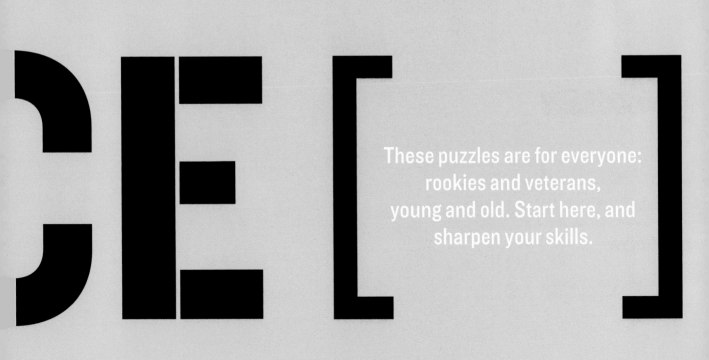

These puzzles are for everyone:
rookies and veterans,
young and old. Start here, and
sharpen your skills.

Spring Awakening

A snowstorm can hide a lot of things, including all our changes

A
—
B
—
C
—
D
—

1   2   3   4   5

8
changes

⧗
2min 0sec

Answers
on page 164

KEEP SCORE ★ ❏ ❏ ❏ ❏ ❏ ❏ ❏ ❏

Is It Art?

Talk among yourselves . . . then solve this puzzle

11
changes
- - - - - - - - -
KEEP
SCORE
❏
❏
❏
❏
❏
❏
❏
❏
❏
❏
❏

⧗

2min 5sec

Answers
on page 164

Cheaper by the Dozen

Here's a bowlful of eggs-cellent twists

A

B

C

D

E

1   2   3   4   5

7
changes
- - - - - - - - -
KEEP
SCORE

❑
❑
❑
❑
❑
❑
❑

⧖
2min 10sec

Answers
on page 164

You Say It's Your Birthday

This party scene is a piece of cake

15
changes

- - - - - - - - -

KEEP
SCORE

☐
☐
☐
☐
☐
☐
☐
☐
☐
☐
☐
☐
☐
☐
☐

⧗

2min 30sec

Answers
on page 164

Wake Up and Smell the Coffee

If you can't beat our best time, you'll be toast

A

—

B

—

C

—

D

—

E

1   2   3   4   5

13
changes

- - - - - - - - -

KEEP
SCORE

❏
❏
❏
❏
❏
❏
❏
❏
❏
❏
❏
❏
❏

⧗

2min 40sec

Answers
on page 164

Clean Sweep

Okay, gang—let's dust off this puzzle

A

B

C

D

E

1 | 2 | 3 | 4 | 5

13
changes
- - - - - - - - -
KEEP
SCORE

⌛
2min 45sec

Answers
on page 164

Short Stuff

This little one is in the pink.
You will be, too, after locating the differences between these photos.

11
changes

KEEP
SCORE

A
—
B
—
C
—
D
—
E

⧗
2min 40sec

Answers
on page 164

1   2   3   4   5

That Can't Be Right

Puzzling while the clock ticks away is
sometimes a weighty matter

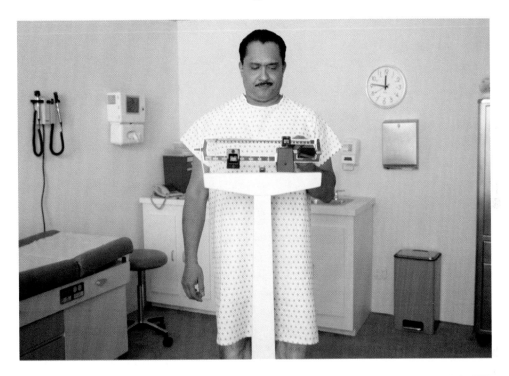

11
changes

KEEP
SCORE

❏
❏
❏
❏
❏
❏
❏
❏
❏
❏

⧗

2min 30sec

Answers
on page 164

A

B

C

D

E

1   2   3   4   5

The MP3 Shuffle

As she grooves to the beat,
her room is changing its tune

A

B

C

D

E

1 | 2 | 3 | 4 | 5

12
changes
- - - - - - - -
KEEP
SCORE

❏
❏
❏
❏
❏
❏
❏
❏
❏
❏
❏
❏

⧗
2min 10sec

Answers
on page 165

Border Patrol

A tip of the sombrero to you if you can figure out this family's transformation

A

B

C

D

E

1   2   3   4   5

16
changes

⧗

2min 50sec

Answers
on page 165

KEEP SCORE ★ ❑ ❑ ❑ ❑ ❑ ❑ ❑ ❑ ❑ ❑ ❑ ❑ ❑ ❑ ❑ ❑ ❑

Magic Squares

We sawed this photo into quarters and floated the pieces around.
Prove your wizardry by levitating them back into place.

Answer
on page 165

0min 30sec

KEEP SCORE

Building Blocks

You can't enter this mall until you
figure out where the door goes

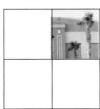

KEEP SCORE

0min 40sec

Answer
on page 165

Strange Fruit

Here's a juicy puzzle that's ripe for the solving

12
changes

⧗
2min 40sec

Answers
on page 165

KEEP SCORE ★ ❏ ❏ ❏ ❏ ❏ ❏ ❏ ❏ ❏ ❏ ❏ ❏

Bored Game

Someone's not taking this game very seriously

A

B

C

D

E

1   2   3   4   5

9
changes

KEEP
SCORE

❏
❏
❏
❏
❏
❏
❏
❏
❏

⌛

2min 55sec

Answers
on page 165

The Playful Playroom

Her world is changing every day.
Can you see how?

A

B

C

D

E

1   2   3   4   5

11
changes

KEEP
SCORE

❏
❏
❏
❏
❏
❏
❏
❏
❏
❏
❏

⧖

3min 25sec

Answers
on page 165

Grease Monkey

It's a dirty puzzle, but somebody's got to solve it.
How about you?

A

B

C

D

E

1   2   3   4   5

10
changes
- - - - - - - - -
KEEP
SCORE

❏
❏
❏
❏
❏
❏
❏
❏
❏
❏

⧖
3min 10sec

Answers
on page 165

Foosball Follies

You won't win if you don't play

A
—
B
—
C
—
D
—
E

1   2   3   4   5

12
changes

⧗
3min 50sec

Answers
on page 165

KEEP SCORE ★ ❑ ❑ ❑ ❑ ❑ ❑ ❑ ❑ ❑ ❑ ❑ ❑

Can You Hear Me Now?

Have a cup of joe and give it a go

10
changes

KEEP
SCORE

❏
❏
❏
❏
❏
❏
❏
❏
❏
❏

⌛
3min 25sec

Answers
on page 166

Vroom, Vroom

Remember, the speed limit is 55 pph (puzzles per hour)

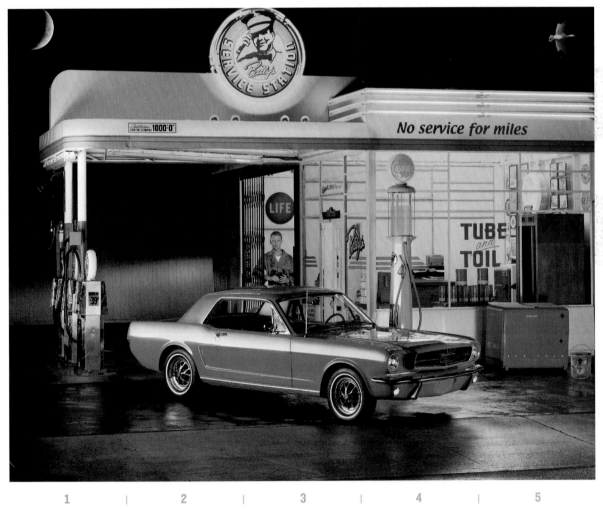

A

B

C

D

E

1   2   3   4   5

18
changes

⏳

4min 15sec

Answers
on page 166

KEEP SCORE ★ ☐☐☐☐☐☐☐☐☐☐☐☐☐☐☐☐☐☐

Leaving on a Jet Plane

Above the tarmac, something's always in the air

12
changes
- - - - - - - - -
KEEP
SCORE

⧗
4min 45sec

Answers
on page 166

A
—
B
—
C
—
D
—
E

1 | 2 | 3 | 4 | 5

May I Have This Dance?

A quick spin around the puzzle below will bring about some changes

12
changes

- - - - - - - -

KEEP
SCORE

4min 40sec

Answers
on page 166

High Score

When you're done visiting this happy pair, try our next section, where things get trickier

17
changes
- - - - - - - - - -
KEEP
SCORE

5min 5sec

Answers
on page 166

MAST

ER[ ]

Here, puzzles get
a little harder. You'll
need to raise
your game a level.

Wheel Fun

Where we'll stop, we don't know

A
—
B
—
C
—
D
—
E

1   2   3   4   5

11
changes

⧗
4min 20sec

Answers
on page 166

KEEP SCORE ★ ❏ ❏ ❏ ❏ ❏ ❏ ❏ ❏ ❏ ❏ ❏ ❏

Shipshape

Let's set sail on this changing sea

A —

B —

C —

D —

E

1 | 2 | 3 | 4 | 5

14
changes
- - - - - - - - -
KEEP
SCORE
❏
❏
❏
❏
❏
❏
❏
❏
❏
❏
❏
❏

⧗
4min 30sec

Answers
on page 166

Bizarre Bazaar

Don't let us pull the rug out
from under you

A
—
B
—
C
—
D
—
E

1 | 2 | 3 | 4 | 5

12
changes

⏳
4min 20sec

Answers
on page 166

KEEP SCORE ★ ❑ ❑ ❑ ❑ ❑ ❑ ❑ ❑ ❑ ❑ ❑ ❑

Cupboard Contest

Something's out of place among these cabinets.
Which one?

1

2

3

4

5

6

0min 30sec

Answer
on page 167

Cubist Pictures

Are all messy desks the same?
Not quite.

1

2

3

4

5

6

0min 35sec

Answer
on page 167

Family Outing

They're ready for some fun in the sun.
Are you?

10
changes

KEEP
SCORE

☐
☐
☐
☐
☐
☐
☐
☐
☐
☐

⌛

3min 50sec

Answers
on page 167

A
—
B
—
C
—
D
—
E

1 | 2 | 3 | 4 | 5

Castles in the Sand

Better hurry
before the clouds roll in

A

—

B

—

C

—

D

—

E

1 | 2 | 3 | 4 | 5

11
changes

- - - - - - - - -

KEEP
SCORE

❑
❑
❑
❑
❑
❑
❑
❑
❑
❑
❑

3min 25sec

Answers
on page 167

Magazine Madness

If you can spot the photo that we've changed here,
it will be a story worth printing

1

2

3

4

5

6

1min 20sec

Answer
on page 167

Oh, You Dolls!

Five of these pictures are exactly the same.
One is just a little different. Can you unlock the puzzle?

1

2

3

4

5

6

0min 45sec

Answer
on page 167

This One's a Gas

Get pumped up and zoom to the finish

12
changes

4min 20sec

Answers
on page 167

KEEP SCORE ★ ❑ ❑ ❑ ❑ ❑ ❑ ❑ ❑ ❑ ❑ ❑ ❑ ❑

Shell Game

Out on the deck, we found some doozies

14
changes
- - - - - - - - -
KEEP
SCORE

❏
❏
❏
❏
❏
❏
❏
❏
❏
❏
❏
❏
❏
❏

⧗

5min 15sec

Answers
on page 167

Just Us Girls

It will be no picnic
finding the 14 changes lurking by the lake

A

B

C

D

E

1   2   3   4   5

14 changes

⧗
4min 20sec

Answers
on page 167

KEEP SCORE ★ ❑❑❑❑❑❑❑❑❑❑❑❑❑❑❑

Three Little Maids

Our alterations here are more than just skin-deep

11
changes
- - - - - - - - -
KEEP
SCORE

❏
❏
❏
❏
❏
❏
❏
❏
❏
❏
❏

⏳

4min 30sec

Answers
on page 167

A

—

B

—

C

—

D

—

E

1 | 2 | 3 | 4 | 5

A Movable Feast

In this puzzle, there's a lot of food for thought

A

–

B

–

C

–

D

–

E

1 | 2 | 3 | 4 | 5

12
changes
- - - - - - - - -
KEEP
SCORE

❏
❏
❏
❏
❏
❏
❏
❏
❏
❏
❏
❏

⌛

4min 45sec

Answers
on page 168

Just Ask for Directions, Okay?

You'll need to, because these wacky signs point every which way

13
changes

- - - - - - - - -

KEEP
SCORE

❏ ❏ ❏ ❏ ❏ ❏ ❏ ❏ ❏ ❏ ❏ ❏ ❏

⧖
6min 5sec

Answers
on page 168

Hole in One

On this street, you'd better proceed with caution

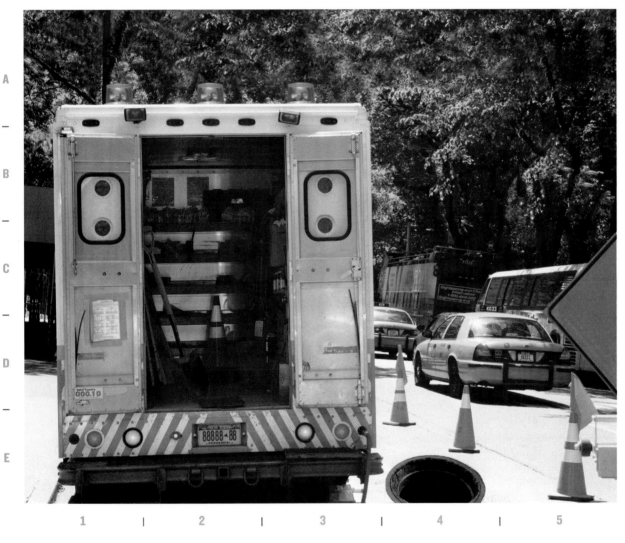

12
changes

⏳

4min 30sec

Answers
on page 168

KEEP SCORE ★ ❏ ❏ ❏ ❏ ❏ ❏ ❏ ❏ ❏ ❏ ❏ ❏

Jumpin' Jack Flash

Use the boxes at the bottom to put
these wild kids in their place

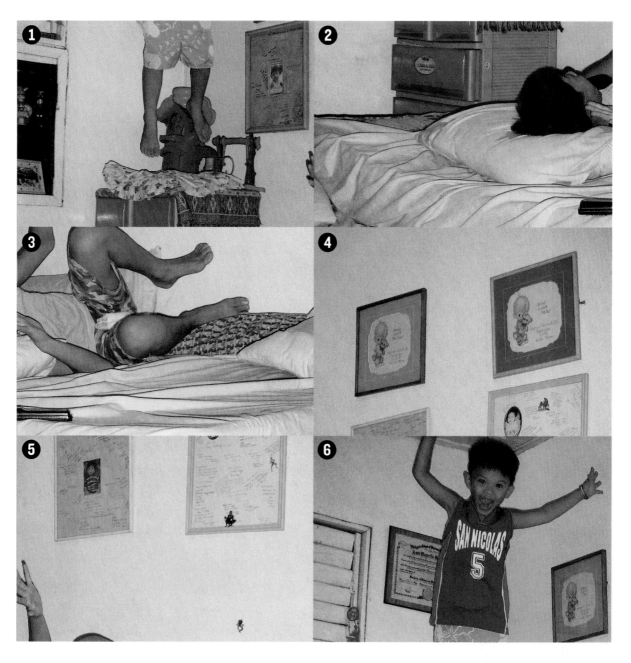

KEEP SCORE

	4
1	5
2	3

Off the Rails

If you can set the pieces of this train station on the right track,
we'll punch your ticket

1min 15sec

Answer
on page 168

Where the Palm Trees Sway

When the wind starts to blow, everything looks different

A

–

B

–

C

–

D

–

E

1 | 2 | 3 | 4 | 5

15
changes

⧖

4min 10sec

Answers
on page 168

KEEP SCORE ★ ❏ ❏ ❏ ❏ ❏ ❏ ❏ ❏ ❏ ❏ ❏ ❏ ❏ ❏ ❏

The Puzzling Pagoda

Negotiating this back alley can be tricky

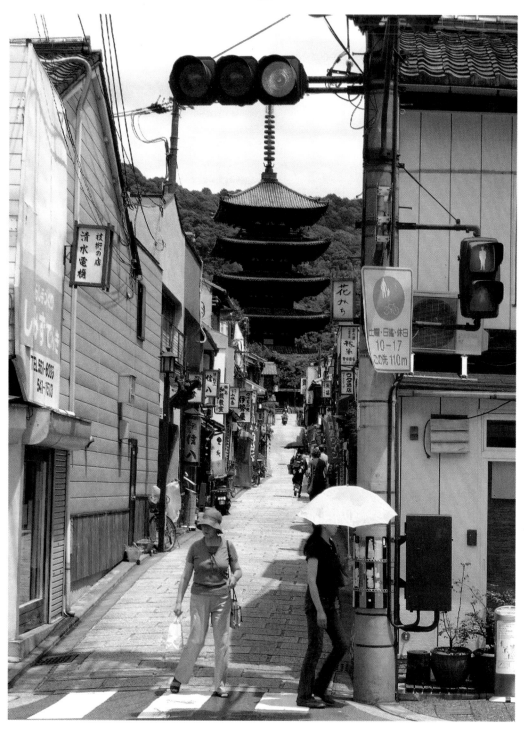

14
changes
- - - - - - - - -
KEEP
SCORE

5min 20sec

Answers
on page 168

Down by the Sea

There's something shady going on here

A
–
B
–
C
–
D
–
E

1 | 2 | 3 | 4 | 5

12
changes

⧗
4min 20sec

Answers
on page 168

KEEP SCORE ★ ❑ ❑ ❑ ❑ ❑ ❑ ❑ ❑ ❑ ❑ ❑ ❑ ❑

Chillin'

While they find this scene restful, you may think it's stressful

5

4

3

2

1

14
changes
- - - - - - - - -
KEEP
SCORE

⧖

6min 5sec

Answers
on page 168

A | B | C | D | E

EXPE

Only serious puzzlers
dare to tread past this point.
Who's in?

King Cotton

Don't bail out when the going gets tough

A

—

B

—

C

—

D

—

E

1 | 2 | 3 | 4 | 5

12
changes

4min 20sec

Answers
on page 169

KEEP SCORE ★

Struttin' Their Stuff

The solution here lies in the balance

A

B

C

D

E

1 | 2 | 3 | 4 | 5

8
changes

- - - - - - - - -

KEEP
SCORE

❏
❏
❏
❏
❏
❏
❏
❏

⏳

5min 30sec

Answers
on page 169

Big Rigs

Wonder who drives the pink truck?

9
changes

- - - - - - - -

KEEP
SCORE

⌛
5min 0sec

Answers
on page 169

A
—
B
—
C
—
D
—
E

1 | 2 | 3 | 4 | 5

Spools Rule

With a bit of concentration, you can sew this up

8
changes

KEEP
SCORE

❑
❑
❑
❑
❑
❑
❑
❑

4min 30sec

Answers
on page 169

Berry Good

Don't let this patch drive you wild

5

4

3

2

1

6
changes

KEEP
SCORE

❏
❏
❏
❏
❏
❏

⌛
5min 35sec

Answers
on page 169

A | B | C | D | E

There's No Place Like . . .

One of these comfy rooms is
unlike all the others

1

2

3

4

5

6

0min 30sec

Answer
on page 169

A Shoe-in

Want to play a little footsie?
Find the photo that's different.

1

2

3

4

5

6

0min 35sec

Answer
on page 169

Raising the Roof

This puzzling building harbors some secrets

A

—

B

—

C

—

D

—

E

1 | 2 | 3 | 4 | 5

9
changes
- - - - - - - -
KEEP
SCORE

❏
❏
❏
❏
❏
❏
❏
❏
❏

⧖
3min 25sec

Answers
on page 169

Ride 'Em Cowboy

Yeehaw, this is fun!

A
B
C
D
E

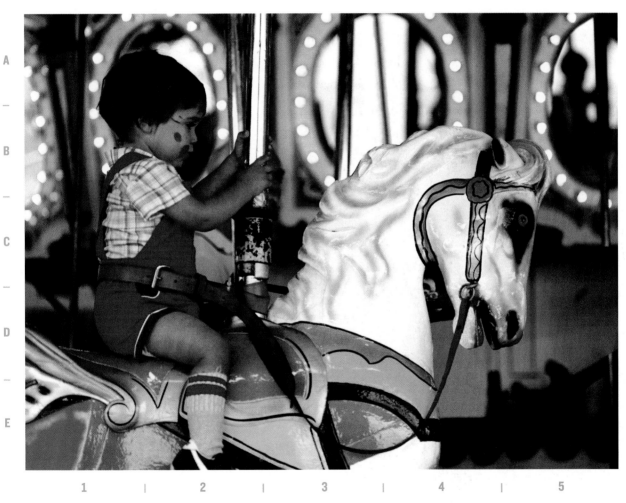

1   2   3   4   5

10
changes

3min 50sec

Answers
on page 169

KEEP SCORE ★ ❑ ❑ ❑ ❑ ❑ ❑ ❑ ❑ ❑ ❑

Stacked Up Over Cleveland

Nothing's very plain about this before-and-after

11
changes
- - - - - - - - -
KEEP
SCORE

❑
❑
❑
❑
❑
❑
❑
❑
❑
❑
❑

⏳

5min 20sec

Answers
on page 169

A New Leaf

Are you ready for the foliage to change?

A
—
B
—
C
—
D
—
E

1   2   3   4   5

6
changes

⌛

3min 50sec

Answers
on page 169

KEEP SCORE ★ ❏ ❏ ❏ ❏ ❏ ❏

Kitchen Renovation

Mom decided to make the place a little livelier

11
changes
- - - - - - - - -
KEEP
SCORE

❏
❏
❏
❏
❏
❏
❏
❏
❏
❏
❏

⏳

5min 40sec

Answers
on page 170

A

B

C

D

E

1 | 2 | 3 | 4 | 5

Bring Chopsticks

The lunch special changes by the minute

14
changes
- - - - - - - - -
KEEP
SCORE

❏
❏
❏
❏
❏
❏
❏
❏
❏
❏
❏
❏
❏
❏

⌛

6min 30sec

Answers
on page 170

A
—
B
—
C
—
D
—
E

1 | 2 | 3 | 4 | 5

Reordering the Closet

Can you clean up this mess?

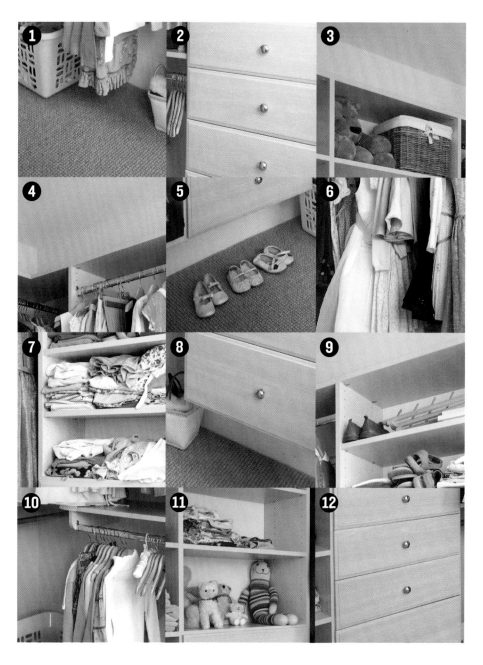

3min 5sec

Answer
on page 170

KEEP SCORE

Wall-to-Wall Fun

Bring order to this colorful chaos and win a prize

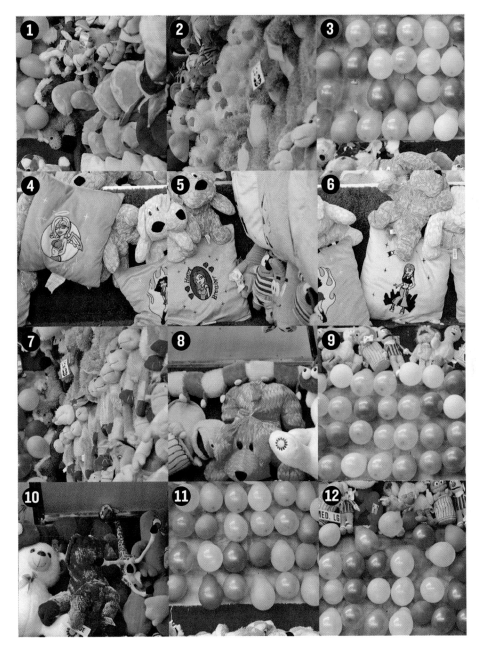

KEEP SCORE

5min 10sec

Answer
on page 170

Wash and Fold

Let's help Dad with the laundry

A

B

C

D

E

1 | 2 | 3 | 4 | 5

8
changes
- - - - - - - - -
KEEP
SCORE

❏
❏
❏
❏
❏
❏
❏
❏

⧗
3min 25sec

Answers
on page 170

Keep the Change

At this diner, you get service with a smile—and a cookie

8
changes

⏳

3min 50sec

Answers
on page 170

Funny Business

He's giving you the third degree (and the ninth)

8
changes
- - - - - - - -
KEEP
SCORE
❏
❏
❏
❏
❏
❏
❏
❏

⧗

3min 25sec

Answers
on page 170

Gone Fishin'

Ponder this lovely, lonely scene by the sea

20
changes

- - - - - - - - -

KEEP
SCORE

❑ ❑ ❑ ❑ ❑ ❑ ❑ ❑ ❑ ❑ ❑ ❑ ❑ ❑ ❑ ❑ ❑ ❑ ❑ ❑

⧗
6min 5sec

Answers
on page 170

A — B — C — D — E

1 — 2 — 3 — 4 — 5

FIRE ISLAND
SAYVILLE, NY

GENIU

JS[ ]

Finding a single difference
in these puzzles is a
challenge. Finding them all
might be impossible.

Not a Creature Was Stirring . . .

Except for the mouse that put this house in disorder

A
B
C
D
E

1   2   3   4   5

Answers on page 176

15 changes

5min 35sec

The Old World

Can you map out everything we've done to this one?

17
changes
- - - - - - - - -
KEEP
SCORE

❑
❑
❑
❑
❑
❑
❑
❑
❑
❑
❑
❑
❑
❑
❑
❑
❑

⧗
4min 45sec

Answers
on page 171

A

B

C

D

E

1   2   3   4   5

Atta Buoy!

We've netted a flotilla of colorful alterations

18
changes

KEEP
SCORE

6min 50sec

Answers
on page 171

1   2   3   4   5

A   B   C   D   E

Puppet Master

This one demands hands-on attention

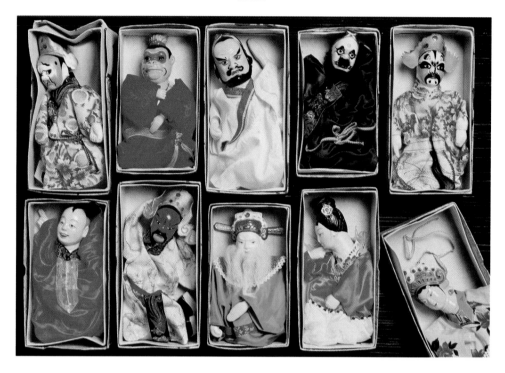

18
changes
- - - - - - - - -
KEEP
SCORE

❏
❏
❏
❏
❏
❏
❏
❏
❏
❏
❏
❏
❏
❏
❏
❏
❏
❏

⏳

6min 5sec

Answers
on page 171

A
B
C
D
E

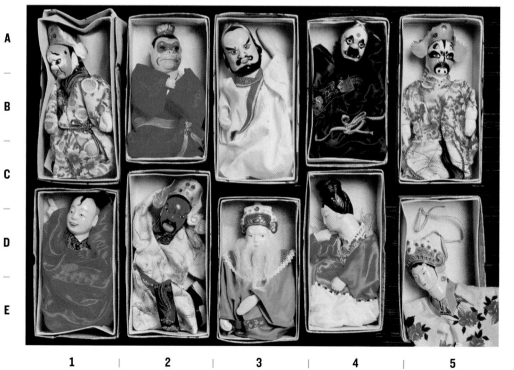

1   2   3   4   5

Pony Up

Find the horse of a different color

14
changes
- - - - - - - -

KEEP
SCORE

❏
❏
❏
❏
❏
❏
❏
❏
❏
❏
❏
❏

5min 25sec

Answers
on page 171

A
—
B
—
C
—
D
—
E

1 | 2 | 3 | 4 | 5

Flower Power

Fixing this picture is a bloomin' ordeal

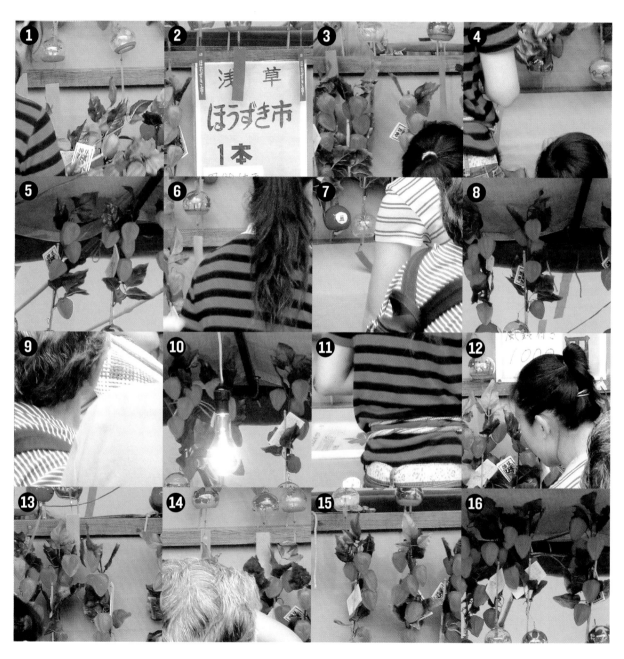

9min 35sec

Answer
on page 171

KEEP SCORE

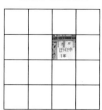

Feeling Lucky?

Bet you can't hit the jackpot quickly

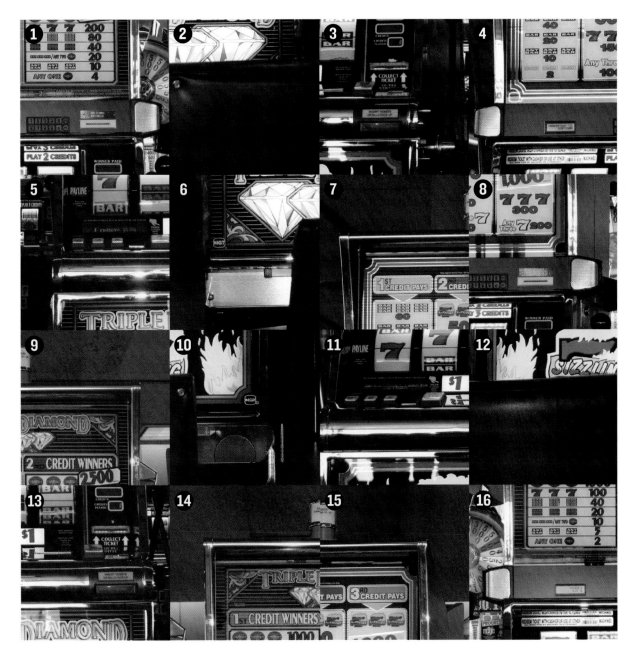

KEEP SCORE

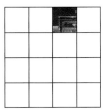

14min 10sec

Answer
on page 171

Where the Heart Is

A sweet scene of domestic bliss conceals some devilish tricks

25
changes

KEEP
SCORE

5min 5sec

Answers
on page 171

ANIMA

LS[   ]

Now some puzzles
starring our fine, feathered
(or furry, or just funny)
friends.

This Can't Be the Caribbean

The march of these penguins is puzzling

5 | 4 | 3 | 2 | 1

A | B | C | D | E

12
changes

KEEP
SCORE

6min 10sec

Answers
on page 171

Come Here Often?

These frogs only have eyes for you, dear

8
changes

- - - - - - - -

KEEP
SCORE

☐
☐
☐
☐
☐
☐
☐
☐

⏳

6min 20sec

Answers
on page 172

A

—

B

—

C

—

D

—

E

1 | 2 | 3 | 4 | 5

Quit Shoving!

Let's horse around at the O.K. Corral

A

B

C

D

E

1   2   3   4   5

11
changes

- - - - - - - - -

KEEP
SCORE

❏
❏
❏
❏
❏
❏
❏
❏
❏
❏
❏

⧗

7min 10sec

Answers
on page 172

Something's Fishy Here

Very strange critters have dived into our tank.
Can you send the party crashers packing?

A
—
B
—
C
—
D
—
E

1   2   3   4   5

14
changes

⧗
—————
5min 10sec

Answers
on page 172

KEEP SCORE ★ ❑ ❑ ❑ ❑ ❑ ❑ ❑ ❑ ❑ ❑ ❑ ❑ ❑ ❑

Hello, Kitties

This puzzle is the cat's meow

A

—

B

—

C

—

D

—

E

1 | 2 | 3 | 4 | 5

12
changes

⏳
4min **50**sec

Answers
on page 172

KEEP SCORE ★ ❏ ❏ ❏ ❏ ❏ ❏ ❏ ❏ ❏ ❏ ❏ ❏

Swanee, How I Love Ya!

Act quickly before these birds take flight

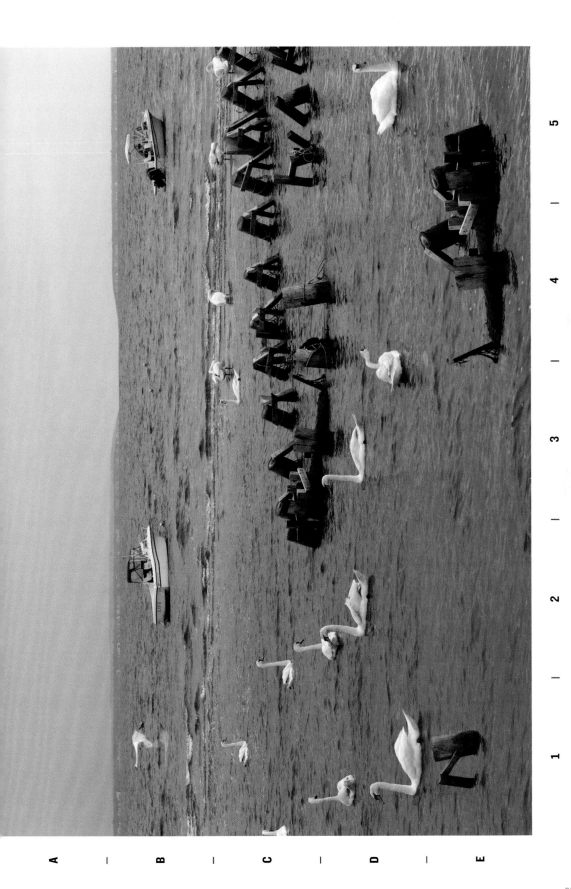

A | B | C | D | E

1 | 2 | 3 | 4 | 5

13
changes
- - - - - - - -
KEEP
SCORE

☐ ☐ ☐ ☐ ☐ ☐ ☐ ☐ ☐ ☐ ☐ ☐ ☐

⏳

4min 45sec

Answers
on page 172

Dog Day Afternoon

They're not supposed to be on the couch, but we're letting them stay

A
—
B
—
C
—
D
—
E

1 | 2 | 3 | 4 | 5

10 changes

⧗

4min 25sec

Answers
on page 172

See-through

The answers are not entirely transparent

6
changes
- - - - - - - -
KEEP
SCORE

❏
❏
❏
❏
❏
❏

⏳

7 min 30 sec

Answers
on page 172

A
—
B
—
C
—
D
—
E

1 | 2 | 3 | 4 | 5

Move Along Now

Something's bound to get these guys running

A

—

B

—

C

—

D

—

E

1 | 2 | 3 | 4 | 5

8
changes

- - - - - - - - -

KEEP
SCORE

❑
❑
❑
❑
❑
❑
❑
❑

⌛

4min 45sec

Answers
on page 172

Back of the Line

Tons of fun await you here

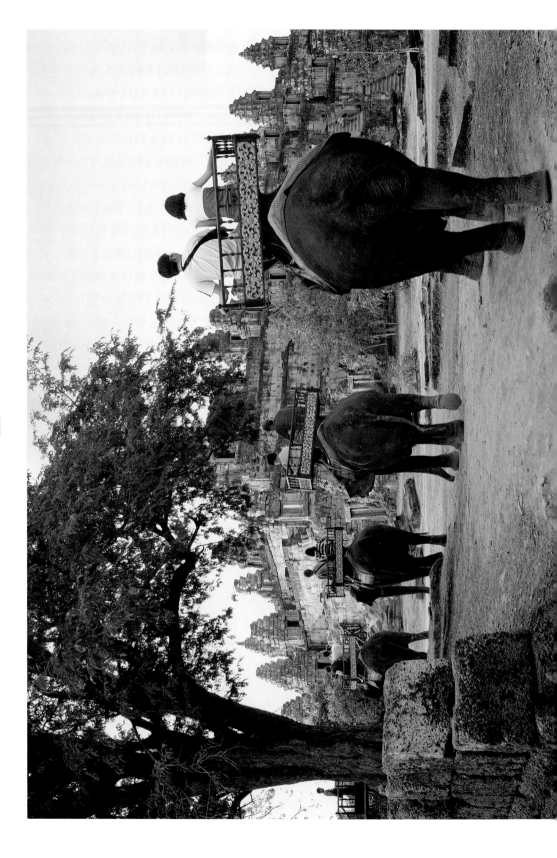

5 | 4 | 3 | 2 | 1

A | B | C | D | E

8
changes

- - - - - - - - -

KEEP
SCORE

☐ ☐ ☐ ☐ ☐ ☐ ☐ ☐

⧗

5min 50sec

Answers
on page 172

LIFE
CLASS

CS[ ]

These puzzles were specially created with memorable photos from the LIFE archives.

Heads A-Poppin'

Is your noggin sharp enough?

A
–
B
–
C
–
D
–
E

1 | 2 | 3 | 4 | 5

12
changes

⏳

6min 10sec

Answers
on page 172

KEEP SCORE ★ ❏ ❏ ❏ ❏ ❏ ❏ ❏ ❏ ❏ ❏ ❏ ❏

The Graduate

You don't have to be Phi Beta Kappa to pass this test

A

—

B

—

C

—

D

—

E

1 | 2 | 3 | 4 | 5

11
changes

- - - - - - - -

KEEP
SCORE

❏
❏
❏
❏
❏
❏
❏
❏
❏
❏
❏

⧗

4min 35sec

Answers
on page 173

Boob Tubes

But you're no boob, right?
So prove it.

13
changes

KEEP
SCORE

A
—
B
—
C
—
D
—
E

⏳

4min 10sec

Answers
on page 173

1 | 2 | 3 | 4 | 5

Shakespeare Slept Here

To play's the thing!

9
changes

KEEP
SCORE

❏
❏
❏
❏
❏
❏
❏
❏
❏

⏳

7min 25sec

Answers
on page 173

Life in the Burbs

Solve it yourself or leave it to Beaver

A
—
B
—
C
—
D
—
E

1 | 2 | 3 | 4 | 5

10
changes
- - - - - - - - -
KEEP
SCORE
❏
❏
❏
❏
❏
❏
❏
❏
❏
❏

⌛
5min 10sec

Answers
on page 173

Haberdashery

Hats off to you for helping these guys out

A — B — C — D — E

1 | 2 | 3 | 4 | 5

11 changes

⧗

3min 20sec

Answers on page 173

KEEP SCORE ★ ❑ ❑ ❑ ❑ ❑ ❑ ❑ ❑ ❑ ❑ ❑

Well Done

Are you eager to dig in?

A

—

B

—

C

—

D

—

E

1 | 2 | 3 | 4 | 5

7
changes
- - - - - - - - -
KEEP
SCORE

❑
❑
❑
❑
❑
❑
❑

⏳
4min 20sec

Answers
on page 173

Not Too Fast, Son

You have to play by the rules of the road

A

B

C

D

E

1   2   3   4   5

10 changes

⧖

5min **10**sec

Answers on page 173

KEEP SCORE ★ ❏ ❏ ❏ ❏ ❏ ❏ ❏ ❏ ❏ ❏

Baggage Claim

Sorting this luggage requires some heavy lifting

14
changes

KEEP
SCORE

❏ ❏ ❏ ❏ ❏ ❏ ❏ ❏ ❏ ❏ ❏ ❏ ❏ ❏

⧖

9min 20sec

Answers
on page 173

ANSWERS

Finished already? Let's see how you did.

[INTRODUCTION]

Page 3: Dancing Fools No. 1 (A2 to B3): The top window has been duplicated. No. 2 (A4): The air conditioner has shimmied to the right. No. 3 (C2 to E2): That plant is going to ruin their rug. No. 4 (C4): He liked her belt so much, now he has his own. No. 5 (D2 to D3): Her hem has been lengthened. No. 6 (D4 to D5): The steam from the radiator must have shrunk it. No. 7 (E1 to E2): The squares have merged to form a mega-diamond. No. 8 (E3 to E4): Hope he doesn't trip on the pillow. No. 9 (E5): Did someone steal the space heater?

[NOVICE]

Page 8: Spring Awakening No. 1 (A3 to B2): Building disappears in blizzard. News at 11. Nos. 2 and 3 (A4 to B4): Where did these windows come from, and should that tulip be tested for steroid use? No. 4 (B2): The flower must be holding its breath. No. 5 (B5): The lights have hopped to the next window. No. 6 (C5): Two new flowers have sprouted. No. 7 (D3 to E2): Hey there, Easter Bunny. No. 8 (E1): That flower has snapped shut.

Page 10: Is It Art? No. 1 (A2): The yellow splotch on her smock has gotten bigger. No. 2 (B1 to C1): Two colorful rows of dots have been added to the picture. No. 3 (B2 to B3): Her fingers are floating in midair. No. 4 (C2 to C5): Yeah, but is it art? No. 5 (D1 to D2): Someone's hungry. No. 6 (D4 to D5): That star is growing. No. 7 (E1 to E2): The scissors have reversed direction. No. 8 (E2): A happy star has risen. No. 9 (E3 to E4): A green crayon has popped up. No. 10 (E4): Is that *M* blushing? No. 11 (E5): The yellow jar of paint has moved.

Page 12: Cheaper by the Dozen No. 1 (A1): Red sleeve, blue sleeve, it's all the same to us. No. 2 (A4): Who has capped that marker? No. 3 (B2): The colors on her sleeve have swapped places. No. 4 (B2 to B3): Is that egg filled with liquor? No. 5 (C3 to C4): The reflection has vanished—maybe it's a clutch of vampire eggs. No. 6 (D1): There's a marker in the grass. No. 7 (D3): That cap isn't chicken, it's just yellow.

Page 14: You Say It's Your Birthday No. 1 (A1 to B2): Her hat has grown. No. 2 (A4 to B4): The yellow balloon is about to burst. No. 3 (A5): Is his hat getting angry? No. 4 (B2): With two hats, she looks positively devilish. Nos. 5 and 6 (B3): His noisemaker has turned blue, and there's an ink stain on his shoulder. No. 7 (B3 to C3): That's where the donkey tail ended up. No. 8 (B4): One of the balloons has turned purple. No. 9 (C3): The Post-it notes have been rearranged to spell out

LIFE. No. 10 (C3 to C4): The monitor has been clipped. No. 11 (D3): That sign makes you wonder what she's got in her cubicle. No. 12 (D4): We heard she likes chocolate cake better. No. 13 (E1 to E3): Now they can never leave the office. Nos. 14 and 15 (E4): The stapler has disappeared, and a pair of scissors has been placed in the basket.

Page 15: Wake Up and Smell the Coffee No. 1 (A1): That tile has been quartered. No. 2 (A1 to B1): Where did the faucet go? No. 3 (A3): What a convenient spot for a switch. No. 4 (A3 to B3): That piece of toast is new. No. 5 (B2 to C2): The butler stabbed the butter with the knife in the kitchen. No. 6 (B3 to C4): There's something strange about that reflection. No. 7 (B5 to D5): You can't have toast without a power cord. No. 8 (C1): Now that there are suds in the sink, someone should do the dishes. No. 9 (C2 to E3): Where did the cutting board go? No. 10 (C2 to C3): The cup of coffee has been refilled. No. 11 (C2 to D2): That slice has been sliced. No. 12 (C3): The knob has turned red. No. 13 (D5 to E4): And the stripes on the towel have become blue.

Page 16: Clean Sweep No. 1 (A1): The clock has crept up the wall. No. 2 (A4): Two horned masks are better than one. No. 3 (B1): Where did that blue mask come from? No. 4 (B4): Nice haircut. No. 5 (B5): A couple of beams have vanished. No. 6 (C1 to D2): She's gone from short-shorts to capris. No. 7 (C2 to D3): The spots on the chair have turned red. No. 8 (C2 to E3): The table and vase add a chic touch. No. 9 (C5): She has changed her top. No. 10 (D2 to E3): The dustpan is now purple. No. 11 (D3): That chair doesn't have a leg to stand on. No. 12 (D4 to E5): Who put down those crazy tiles? No. 13 (D5): That popcorn is going to spill.

Page 18: Short Stuff No. 1 (A1 to B2): The painting has doubled in size. No. 2 (A4): The doorway can now accommodate the extra tall. No. 3 (B2): The hearts on her chest have traded places. No. 4 (C1 to D1): Celery is the new orchid this season. No. 5 (C2): What happened to the cactus? No. 6 (C4): Someone has padlocked the door. No. 7 (C5): *Mmm*, lemonade. No. 8 (D2 to D3): That rubber band ball has grown. No. 9 (D3 to E5): The folder has turned orange. No. 10 (E1): Two hearts have been stamped on that piece of paper. No. 11 (E3): The pen has vanished.

Page 19: That Can't Be Right No. 1 (A2): The glove dispenser has inched upward. Nos. 2 and 3 (A3): He's dyed his hair and shaved his mustache. No. 4 (A4 to B4): That's a huge clock. No. 5 (A5 to E5): The cabinet has vanished. No. 6 (B3): A plunging neckline on a hospital gown is quite risqué. No. 7 (B3 to C3): He has gained a lot of weight. No. 8 (B4 to C5): The paper towel dispenser has flipped its lid. No. 9 (D3): Part of the scale has been obscured. No. 10 (D5 to E5): The trash can has turned red. No. 11 (E3): The hem of his gown has been let out.

Page 20: The MP3 Shuffle No. 1 (A1): She must like him best—his picture has been enlarged and moved to a better spot. No. 2 (A3 to B2): No earbuds, no cord, no music. No. 3 (A3): The stripes on his shirt have turned orange. No. 4 (A5 to B5): Her friends are now standing on their heads. No. 5 (B4): When you get it going, that lava lamp is pretty colorful. No. 6 (B4 to C5): She needs to hit the books. No. 7 (C1 to C2): The cat's name is Zacky. No. 8 (C5 to D5): That's a big wastebasket. No. 9 (D2 to D3): Her pant leg has lost its cuff. No. 10 (D3 to E3): Is she old enough for tattoos? No. 11 (D3 to D4): We like that backpack better in yellow. No. 12 (E2): And we really, really dig the new shoe hue.

Page 22: Border Patrol No. 1 (A4 to B4): His hat has been supersized. No. 2 (B1): A mask has appeared from the shadows. No. 3 (B2 to D2): That's a pretty pink dress. No. 4 (B3): One balloon has changed its color. No. 5 (B3 to C4): Her hat now matches her sister's. No. 6 (B4 to C5): He looks good in blue. No. 7 (B5 to D5): Someone has bricked up the doorway. No. 8 (C2 to D3): Is that a mood hat? No. 9 (C3 to C4): Her sweater has turned yellow. No. 10 (C5): That maraca will help Dad keep the beat. No. 11 (C5 to D5): The color scheme of that blanket has been altered. Nos. 12 and 13 (D5): A Mexican skull is stalking them, and the green hat band is on the move. Nos. 14 and 15 (E2): The bags have switched tints, and Mom has slipped on some cool boots. No. 16 (E5): His shoe is sole-less.

Page 24: Magic Squares

4	3
2	1

Page 25: Building Blocks

3	1
2	4

Page 26: Strange Fruit No. 1 (A2 to B2): That pink wrapper is apparently contagious. No. 2 (A3): The cactus is really blooming. No. 3 (A3 to B4): A giant melon has joined the group. Nos. 4 and 5 (A5): The reflection of someone's torso has appeared, and the orange shelf has turned green. No. 6 (C4): Those apples are piling up. No. 7 (D2): Where did that red apple come from? No. 8 (D3 to E4): The grocer is really eager to sell those nectarines.

No. 9 (D5): More grapefruit stickers have cropped up. No. 10 (E1): A bunch of strawberries is trying to crowd out the tomatoes. No. 11 (E2 to E4): Those two signs have switched their prices. No. 12 (E5): A few rogue grapefruits are attacking the peaches.

Page 28: Bored Game No. 1 (B2): The center diamond has turned gray. No. 2 (B2 to B4): You can't sit there anymore. No. 3 (B5): That bench is a lawsuit waiting to happen. No. 4 (C2): A new puck has joined the game. No. 5 (C2 to C5): The court has expanded. No. 6 (C4 to C5): The white diamonds on her socks have become blue. No. 7 (D2 to D3): OFF has been switched ON. No. 8 (D4 to D5): One puck has changed its color. No. 9 (E4 to E5): The 7 is now 11 times bigger.

Page 30: The Playful Playroom No. 1 (A1): Prices must be going up—the cash register display has been enlarged. No. 2 (A3): The letter *B* has been lowercased. No. 3 (A4): Peekaboo, I see you. No. 4 (A4 to A5): Someone has carved a new line on the shelf. No. 5 (A5): That's a lovely butterfly. No. 6 (B5): A stack of books has been left behind. No. 7 (C3 to C4): What's in the extra basket? No. 8 (C4 to C5): A bear has taken over that spot. No. 9 (D2 to E2): She has rolled up her sock. No. 10 (D4): The shelves have lost some support. No. 11 (D4 to E5): It must be a flying carpet, seeing as it's disappeared.

Page 32: Grease Monkey No. 1 (A5): The clock has moved over. Nos. 2 and 3 (B2 to B3): He has grown a mustache and lost the T-shirt. No. 4 (B4 to C4): That plant should suck up the excess carbon dioxide around here. No. 5 (C1): The NO SMOKING sign has jumped to the left. No. 6 (C2 to D2): The stripes have changed color. No. 7 (C4 to D4): A red handle stands out better. No. 8 (C5): The fire extinguisher sign has been flipped. No. 9 (E3): The yellow stripe has vanished. No. 10 (E5): The blue bricks now extend to the floor.

Page 34: Foosball Follies No. 1 (A2): It has gotten a little harder to reach the phone. No. 2 (A4): A blue star has been added to the lineup. No. 3 (A4 to A5): The giant red star has duplicated itself. No. 4 (A5 to B5): Someone has turned on the light. No. 5 (B1 to C1): The blue shirt has gone from plain to ornate. No. 6 (B4 to C5): This sweater suits her outfit better. No. 7 (C2): The moon is rising on that poster. No. 8 (C2 to D2): A statue has crashed the party. No. 9 (D3 to D4): A plastic player has dropped out of the game. No. 10 (D5): Cute puppy. No. 11 (E1 to E2): The Foosball table has gained an extra slot. No. 12 (E3): What happened to the handle?

Page 36: **Can You Hear Me Now?** No. 1 (A1 to B1): The green curtain has taken over. No. 2 (B3 to B4): That trumpet should get her attention. No. 3 (B5 to C4): How can that watch remain around her neck if half the chain is missing? No. 4 (C4 to D5): She's pulled down her sweater. Nos. 5 and 6 (D3): The table has earned more stripes, and someone has scarfed up the pastry. No. 7 (D4): She's finished the coffee, too. No. 8 (E1 to E2): That's a funny place for a coffee cup. No. 9 (E2 to E3): Will she click her ruby slippers? No. 10 (E3): The rug has been cleaned too well at that spot.

Page 38: ***Vroom, Vroom*** No. 1 (A1): It's a waxing moon. No. 2 (A2 to A3): The station sign has moved to the right. No. 3 (A4 to B5): The neon strip light has tripled. No. 4 (A5): The silly goose has reversed direction. Nos. 5 and 6 (B2): The caution sign has shifted to the left, and the clearance height has been cubed. No. 7 (B2 to B3): You'll be better able to spot the changes with four spotlights. No. 8 (B4 to B5): If you need to use the restroom, you'd better do so now. No. 9 (B4 to C4): The gas tank has turned yellow. No. 10 (C4): And it's three-quarters full. Nos. 11 and 12 (C3): Our logo has shown up above the mechanic, who's making another appearance in this book. No. 13 (C4 to C5): Now offering tube and toil. No. 14 (C4 to D4): More cans have been added to the display. No. 15 (D1): If only gas cost this little. Nos. 16 and 17 (D5): Where did that blue ice chest come from, and who left that green can outside? No. 18 (E4): It's a wonder that car's still standing.

Page 40: **Leaving on a Jet Plane** No. 1 (A2 to B2): That's a tall control tower. No. 2 (A3): Hot air balloons should not fly so close to an airport. No. 3 (A5 to B4): Can that plane operate without a tail? No. 4 (A5 to B5): Hey, buddy—that's a restricted area. No. 5 (B1): Is someone supposed to be on that walkway? No. 6 (B4): The sign has reversed hues. Nos. 7 and 8 (C3): The guy under the wing has disappeared, and the nose of the plane has turned white. No. 9 (D1): The yellow pipe has moved up in the world. No. 10 (D3 to E3): And a blue pipe has taken its place. No. 11 (E1 to E3): One of the workmen has cloned himself twice. No. 12 (E4 to E5): An extra yellow stripe has been added.

Page 41: **May I Have This Dance?** No 1 (A2): The warning sign has headed stage left. No. 2 (A5): A pink balloon has popped up. No. 3 (B4 to D5): Her dress is now red. No. 4 (B5): Her head scarf has turned purple. No. 5 (C2): His shirtsleeve is growing. No. 6 (C5 to E5): She's wearing some groovy slacks. No. 7 (D1 to E1): His pants have been star struck. No. 8 (D2 to D3): Her dress has become more demure. No. 9 (E1 to E2): Got milk? No. 10 (E1 to E5): The stripe on the floor has changed color. No. 11 (E3): She'd better put on her flip-flop before she hits the dance floor. No. 12 (E3 to E4): The chair's reflection has disappeared.

Page 42: **High Score** Nos. 1 and 2 (A4): That keyhole has gotten so big that it has sunk and taken the top of the door with it. No. 3 (B3): She has swapped her controller for a drill. No. 4 (B5): They're looking at our second puzzle book on-screen. No. 5 (C1 to C2): She has taken off her bracelet. No. 6 (C2 to D3): Her controller is now wireless. No. 7 (C4 to D5): Without legs, that foot stool is going to come crashing down. Nos. 8 and 9 (C5): One of the flowers on the stool has grown, and someone has filled the glass. No. 10 (D1): That leg is broken. No. 11 (D2): The accordion should keep the monkey happy. No. 12 (D3): A banana has appeared under the couch. Nos. 13 and 14 (D4): She got a tribal Pac-Man tattoo, and her shoe has turned gray. No. 15 (D5): The grapes have reddened. Nos. 16 and 17 (D5 to E5): The rug has receded, and there's a tool bag on it. Maybe that's where she found the drill.

[MASTER]

Page 46: **Wheel Fun** No. 1 (A3 to B3): The green car has turned purple. No. 2 (B1 to B2): Stop the ride—the yellow car has disappeared. Nos. 3 and 4 (B1 to C2): The lightbulbs have fled the dome, and the blue diamonds look flushed. No. 5 (B4 to C5): The roof has gone from red to blue. No. 6 (C4): The green car may soon share the yellow car's fate. No. 7 (C5): That car is moving so fast that its numbers have flown off. No. 8 (D1 to E1): With such a large crack in the support beam, it's surprising that the whole ride hasn't fallen over. No. 9 (D4): So much for safety bars. Nos. 10 and 11 (E3): SOUTH has been flipped upside down, and the 17 is down 10.

Page 48: **Shipshape** No. 1 (A3 to B3): The center mast has been lengthened. No. 2 (A3 to A4): The sail is now tipped with green. No. 3 (B1 to B2): Some more clouds have rolled in. No. 4 (C1): The island across the bay has grown larger. No. 5 (C3): Is that an extra eye? No. 6 (C4 to C5): Two windsurfers have sailed into view. No. 7 (D1 to E1): A few of the shadows have vanished. No. 8 (D2 to D4): Red stripes have been added to the outrigger arms. No. 9 (D3): There are three new dots on the mast. No. 10 (D4): That bar has become bluer. No. 11 (D5): The white pole has disappeared. No. 12 (E2): She's smiling now. No. 13 (E2 to E3): And her eye has moved down. No. 14 (E3): Someone has taken the wooden block.

Page 50: **Bizarre Bazaar** No. 1 (A2 to B3): Two pots have switched places. No. 2 (B1 to B5): The awning has been repainted blue. No. 3 (C1): That cross has become a star. No. 4 (C2 to D2): The blanket has slipped behind the saddle. No. 5 (C3): The girl in the middle is happy now. Nos. 6, 7, and 8 (C4): The boy has moved a rung up the ladder and lost his watch, and those peppers have been kicked up a notch. No. 9 (D5): Someone has left the Virgin Mary on top of the rugs. No. 10 (E1): Watch your step. No. 11 (E2): A new bird has flown onto the blanket. No. 12 (E3 to E4): A yellow stripe has been added to the street.

Page 52: Cupboard Contest The little partridge has flown off photo No. 5.

Page 53: Cubist Pictures In photo No. 3, he has to pick up the *cat*.

Page 54: Family Outing No. 1 (A5): The window now has curtains. No. 2 (B1 to C1): The street sign has been towed. No. 3 (B2): A handle will make it easier to open the trunk. No. 4 (B4): He looks fetching with that flower behind his ear. No. 5 (B4 to B5): Someone has rolled up the window on the driver's side. No. 6 (C3): She must have dropped her hat. No. 7 (C4): Without a keyhole, you can't lock the door. No. 8 (D1 to E1): The suitcase has gotten longer. No. 9 (D3 to E5): The grass is always greener under the car. No. 10 (D4): The umbrella has been stretched.

Page 55: Castles in the Sand Nos. 1 and 2 (A2 to A3): The clouds are billowing out of control, and Mama's got a brand-new hat. No. 3 (B2 to B3): She's got a one-piece bathing suit, too. No. 4 (C3 to D3): The boy's pail has spent a little too much time in the sun. No. 5 (C4): The umbrella's pole has vanished. No. 6 (C4 to D5): The daisies on her suit have tanned. Nos. 7 and 8 (C5): The straw tote has disappeared, and the red bag has sprouted more diamonds. No. 9 (D1 to E1): An extra turret always comes in handy. No. 10 (D3 to E4): Bigger is better, especially when it comes to castles. No. 11 (E5): A pillar of sand is missing.

Page 56: Magazine Madness In photo No. 4, *The Country Gentleman* has moved to the fore.

Page 57: Oh, You Dolls! That dapper doll in the middle of photo No. 5 has been replaced by a trio of nesters.

Page 58: This One's a Gas No. 1 (A1 to A5): The edge of the roof is kind of blue. Nos. 2 and 3 (A1 to B1): The hose has been lengthened, and the tea kettle has done an about-face. No. 4 (A2): The ladder is missing a rung. No. 5 (A4 to B5): GRAPETTE has lost a *T.* Nos. 6 and 7 (B2): The station now sells feet, and the *O* has fallen out of GASOLINE. Nos. 8 and 9 (B3): PHILLIPS 66 is up 33, and someone has turned on the light. No. 10 (C3): You won't need glasses anymore to read that sign. No. 11 (C4): Apparently, you can smoke here, but we wouldn't recommend it. No. 12 (C5 to D5): That triangle has flipped over CONOCO.

Page 60: Shell Game Nos. 1 and 2 (A1): Two nails have popped up, and that rock has earned more stripes. Nos. 3 and 4 (B2 to B3): The orange-and-white shell has flipped up, and the wee purple shell has vanished. No. 5 (B5): Another starfish has appeared on deck. No. 6 (B5 to C5): That white fella is inching forward. No. 7 (C1): The spiral shell has rotated 90 degrees. No. 8 (D1): The nail has disappeared. No. 9 (D2 to E2): The butterfly has gained more spots. No. 10 (D4 to D5): That guy needs to go on a diet. Nos. 11 and 12 (E4): A conch has joined the party, and two planks have joined forces. Nos. 13 and 14 (E5): The sea glass is now a lovely shade of grayish blue, and we've seen that stone before.

Page 62: Just Us Girls No. 1 (A2 to A3): The branch has grown. No. 2 (B2): A canoeist has paddled into this puzzle. No. 3 (B4): Her hairdo has gotten poufier. No. 4 (C2 to C3): Seeds have sprouted on her shirt. No. 5 (C3): The cup has turned yellow. Nos. 6 and 7 (C4): Her shirt has gone from red to blue. Is that because she's sad to see that slice of watermelon on the table? No. 8 (D1): Hey, pick up that cup. No. 9 (D1 to D2): Her suit has been stretched down to her thighs. No. 10 (D2 to E3): The grass is invading the cement's turf. No. 11 (D3 to E3): The table has lost a leg. No. 12 (E4): The basket is now seedless. Nos. 13 and 14 (E5): Did the finch peck off the heel of her shoe?

Page 64: Three Little Maids No. 1 (B1 to C5): They've raised the roof. Nos. 2 and 3 (B4 to C5): The clock has moved to the right, and the 6 has been turned upside down. No. 4 (C1): *Aww,* she's lost a heart. No. 5 (C5 to D5): An extra window has been added. Nos. 6 and 7 (D4): That fickle necklace has found a new girl to charm, and her face looks eerily familiar. No. 8 (D5 to E5): A window has vanished. No. 9 (E1): The hem of her skirt has been let out. No. 10 (E2): The bottom of the middle girl's cone is now green. No. 11 (E3 to E4): And the bottom of the pink cone has fallen off.

Page 66: A Movable Feast No. 1 (A1 to A2): That picture is worth at least one more feast. No. 2 (A3): Half of the wooden beam has vanished. No. 3 (B1 to B2): We recommend the merlot this evening. No. 4 (B2 to B3): That banana has ripened. No. 5 (B5): A frog has hopped onto the bottle. Nos. 6 and 7 (C3): The pestle is gone, but we have more thyme. No. 8 (C5): And you thought a towel couldn't change its stripes. Nos. 9 and 10 (D1): Some ants have invaded, and the cinnamon stick has been broken in two. No. 11 (D3 to D4): Here's a cooking tip: Less lime is more. No. 12 (E5): Double the peppers, double the fun!

Page 68: Just Ask for Directions, Okay? No. 1 (A2): The street light has flown up. No. 2 (B1 to B2): Germantown has become Chestertown. No. 3 (B4): That light is sending mixed messages. No. 4 (B5): TURN has swapped places with RED. No. 5 (C1): A tiny car is driving along that sign structure as if it were a bridge. No. 6 (C1 to D1): What a tall hazard sign. No. 7 (C3): This way to Germany. Nos. 8 and 9 (C4): An SUV is being tailed by its twin, and all arrows point to New Jersey. Nos. 10 and 11 (D3): You can take either road to get on the turnpike, and the brake light has been placed above the rearview mirror. No. 12 (D3 to E4): The passenger has left. Was it something he said? No. 13 (D4): The guy in the dark blue sedan has changed his mind about where he wants to go.

Page 70: Hole in One No. 1 (A1): The pole has vanished. No. 2 (A1 to A3): The situation has been upgraded to a three-light emergency. No. 3 (B1): He'd better not back up the truck without that mirror. No. 4 (B5): The flag has flown the coop. No. 5 (C1 to C3): The reflectors have doubled. No. 6 (C2 to D2): A shovel might come in handy in this line of work. No. 7 (C4): The sightseeing bus has three extra lights. No. 8 (C5 to D5): Men (no longer) at work. No. 9 (D5): That taxi driver is in wheel trouble. No. 10 (E1 to E3): Who turned on the lights? Nos. 11 and 12 (E4): The cone has lost a stripe. Maybe it got sucked into that gaping manhole.

Page 72: Jumpin' Jack Flash

6	4
1	5
2	3

Page 73: Off the Rails

4	3
5	1
6	2

Page 74: Where the Palm Trees Sway No. 1 (A3): The wind has changed direction. No. 2 (A3 to B3): One of the trees has shot up. No. 3 (B2): A baby cloud has engulfed part of that branch. Nos. 4 and 5 (C5): The lamppost has been shortened, and its finial has vanished. No. 6 (D1): The speed limit is now zero. No. 7 (D2): A blue umbrella is blushing. Nos. 8 and 9 (D2 to E2): A sign has disappeared, while that man has dropped in. No. 10 (D3): A cruise ship has come in. No. 11 (D3 to E3): He's got it made in the shade. No. 12 (D4 to E4): The speed limit here is 30 mph. Nos. 13 and 14 (E1): A puddle has appeared, and her shorts have turned red. No. 15 (E1 to E3): The sidewalk has been widened.

Page 76: The Puzzling Pagoda No. 1 (A2): The red light has shifted left. Nos. 2 and 3 (A3): What does it mean to lose a spire but gain a floor? No. 4 (A4 to A5): Extra ridges have been added to the wall. No. 5 (B1): Does that sign mean the same thing upside down? No. 6 (B4 to C5): The street light is floating in midair. No. 7 (B5 to C5): Blue means walk. No. 8 (C2): The boxes have been removed from the wall. No. 9 (C3 to D3): The woman with the hat has a twin. No. 10 (C4): Somebody has translated that sign. No. 11 (D2): The top half of the door has been erased. No. 12 (D2 to E3): She's switched positions. No. 13 (E1 to E2): Two crosswalk stripes have merged. No. 14 (E5): The container has vanished.

Page 78: Down by the Sea Nos. 1 and 2 (B1): The cruise ship has changed directions, and the small boat it was towing has disappeared. No. 3 (B1 to C1): The sea has swallowed up a few umbrellas. No. 4 (B4): What is that colorful misshapen lump, and why has it moved? No. 5 (B5): The gull has hopped from one roof to the next. No. 6 (C1): The umbrella stripes have gone from red to blue. No. 7 (C2): The green cloth has picked a new door to hang itself on. No. 8 (C5): The 24 has been duplicated. No. 9 (D1 to D2): Guess the lady decided to head out. No. 10 (D3): That one flower is all blue. No. 11 (E1 to E2): One of the umbrellas has changed its stripe. No. 12 (E3 to E5): All the blue squares have solidified.

Page 80: Chillin' No. 1 (A1): The railing is missing. No. 2 (A2): Stop, shirt thief! No. 3 (A4 to A5): The fence has disappeared. No. 4 (B1): That hose is broken. No. 5 (B3): The bucket has gotten a nasty sunburn. No. 6 (B3 to C4): They've switched places. No. 7 (B4 to C5): The thief has also run off with the bike. No. 8 (B5 to D5): The umbrella stripes have turned greenish yellow. No. 9 (C1): A ball has bounced onto the scene. No. 10 (C3): He's logging in. No. 11 (C4): The flip-flops have flipped-flopped over there. No. 12 (D1 to E1): Two planks have been fused together. No. 13 (D2): The spray nozzle has shifted to the right. No. 14 (D5 to E5): Where did the umbrella stand go?

Page 84: **King Cotton** Nos. 1 and 2 (B2): A few lights and a bar have been added to the top of the cotton-pickin' cab. No. 3 (B3 to C3): The hydraulic rods have vanished. Nos. 4 and 5 (B4): An extra light has appeared on top of the harvester's cab, and the exhaust valve has been blown away. No. 6 (B5): Taller antennas get better reception. No. 7 (C1): The harvesting arm has been extended to the left. Nos. 8 and 9 (C4): The harvester has lost a panel—and an operator. Nos. 10 and 11 (C5): A safety light has popped up on that bar, and more cotton has appeared on the horizon. No. 12 (D4 to D5): They forgot to harvest this row.

Page 86: **Struttin' Their Stuff** No. 1 (A1 to B2): Three windows have merged to form a mega-window. No. 2 (A2): The roof has been extended. No. 3 (B1 to E2): That guy must be eating his Wheaties. No. 4 (B3): His hat has lost its pom-pom. No. 5 (B5 to C5): Where did the crane go? No. 6 (D2 to E2): That patch of white bricks is down two rows. No. 7 (E3): That clown better watch his step—his stilt has shrunk. No. 8 (E4 to E5): The paving stones have been halved.

Page 88: **Big Rigs** No. 1 (A5 to B5): The exhaust pipe has shot up. No. 2 (B3 to C3): Parking should be easier with that extra street-lamp. No. 3 (C1 to D1): The red cab has replaced the silver SUV. Nos. 4 and 5 (C2): The hill is bulging upward, and half the pole has disappeared. No. 6 (C4): That exhaust pipe has changed direction. No. 7 (D2 to E3): Those trucks have swapped hub caps. No. 8 (D5): Hey, buddy, can you spare a headlight? No. 9 (E5): The truck now belongs to LIFE.

Page 89: **Spools Rule** No. 1 (B1 to C3): The chair has wheeled off. No. 2 (B2): You can't turn on a light without a switch. No. 3 (B2 to B5): And how can the light stay up without its support arm? No. 4 (C1): Someone has slapped a label on that spool. No. 5 (C3 to D3): That beige one has lost its center. No. 6 (C3 to C4): One of the lilac spools has grown taller. No. 7 (D1 to E1): Oh, the yellow spool of Texas. No. 8 (E2 to E5): The table edge has disappeared.

Page 90: **Berry Good** No. 1 (A4): A blueberry has cropped up. No. 2 (B3): And a red one has too. No. 3 (B4 to C5): That guy has made like Violet Beauregarde and blown up. No. 4 (C2): That blueberry has turned over. No. 5 (C5 to E5): Who knew that leaves could move? No. 6 (D3 to D4): Hey, put that berry back.

Page 92: **There's No Place Like . . .** Who took the cane out of photo No. 6?

Page 93: **A Shoe-in** The brown sandal in photo No. 5 has shifted down.

Page 94: **Raising the Roof** No. 1 (A1): The horn above the porch is stretching skyward. No. 2 (A3): And the horn atop the roof has turned right. No. 3 (A5 to B5): That protrusion aloft the eave has taken off. No. 4 (B1 to D5): The porch's roof has been lowered. No. 5 (C5): Another window means more light. No. 6 (D1): The light blue flag has doubled in size. No. 7 (D4 to E4): One of the back pillars has vanished. No. 8 (D4): One of the light green flags has turned blue. No. 9 (E2): That column has moved closer to the house.

Page 96: **Ride 'Em Cowboy** No. 1 (A1): A bulb has vanished. No. 2 (B2): The green spot on his face has turned red—hope it's not anything serious. No. 3 (B5): His reflection has hopped from the middle mirror to the last one. No. 4 (C5): Now the horse can see where he's going. No. 5 (C5 to D5): A large shadow has been cast across that pole. No. 6 (D4): His full-on whinny has become a mere whimper. No. 7 (D4 to E4): The horse next to him has galloped into the sunset. No. 8 (E1): The yellow panel has turned purple. No. 9 (E2): His sock has lost a stripe. No. 10 (E3): The stirrup is gone.

Page 98: **Stacked Up Over Cleveland** No. 1 (A3): The gyroscope is missing part of its shaft. No. 2 (A4): The yellow arrow has turned blue. No. 3 (B1): The computer key has reversed direction. No. 4 (B2 to B3): *X* marks the spot. No. 5 (B5): The tarot card has been altered. No. 6 (C1 to D2): Our logo is popping up everywhere. No. 7 (C4): The typewriter key has lost its letter. No. 8 (D3 to E3): The 6 and 7 have swapped places. No. 9 (D4): The *N* has become an *M*. No. 10 (E2): Another yellow plane has landed. No. 11 (E5): The needle on one of those dials has rotated 90 degrees.

Page 100: **A New Leaf** No. 1 (A2): A vein has been stripped from that leaf. No. 2 (A4 to B5): The midrib is missing. No. 3 (B2 to C2): In this case, *AWOL* means "absent without leaf." No. 4 (D2): Well, some lucky bug had a snack. No. 5 (D3 to D4): The golden leaf has edged out the rust-colored one. No. 6 (D5 to E5): That leaf has gotten a little green.

ANSWERS

Page 102: Kitchen Renovation No. 1 (A1 to B1): Would you like a balloon with your sandwich? No. 2 (B1 to C2): The cup has been supersized. No. 3 (B2 to C2): Get those dirty bottles out of that clean kitchen. No. 4 (B4 to B5): Someone has eaten the peppers. No. 5 (B5): A butterfly is sampling the fruit. No. 6 (C2): If you don't want the balloon, would you like an apple instead? No. 7 (C3): The bottom of the vase has vanished. No. 8 (C3 to E4): The towel is kind of blue. No. 9 (C5): The fruit bowl has lost its reflection. No. 10 (D5 to E5): That stool has been taking its vitamins. No. 11 (E3): Be sure not to sit on that cup of coffee.

Page 103: Bring Chopsticks No. 1 (A1): They've added a slice of tuna sushi to that dish. Nos. 2 and 3 (A3): The title of that entree has been changed, and a bowl of rice has mushroomed. No. 4 (A4): Are you going to eat those tomatoes? No. 5 (A5 to B5): The sign has been turned upside down. No. 6 (A5): The scallions have formed a ghostly face on that gelatinous mass. No. 7 (C1 to D1): A little Tabasco has been mixed into the miso soup. No. 8 (C2 to C3): There's a new bowl in town. No. 9 (C3 to C4): The sign has been enlarged for your viewing pleasure. No. 10 (C4): Hey, bring back the beer. No. 11 (D2): That must be the dirty rice. No. 12 (D3): The fish cakes have sprouted tails. No. 13 (E3): The title of that dish has been altered. No. 14 (E4 to E5): The serving board has grown larger.

Page 104: Reordering the Closet

3	4	9
11	6	7
12	10	2
5	1	8

Page 105: Wall-to-Wall Fun

8	10	2
9	12	7
3	11	1
4	6	5

Page 106: Wash and Fold No. 1 (A2 to A3): How is that shirt staying up? No. 2 (A5): The collar of the jersey has dropped its stitches. No. 3 (B3 to B4): Dad's shirt has lost its thin stripe. No. 4 (B5): The two-barrette look is *so* last year. No. 5 (B5 to C5): Some of the stripes on that towel have been washed out. No. 6 (C1 to E3): That dryer is no longer a front-loader. No. 7 (D1): His sandal decided to take a hike. No. 8 (E2 to E4): Dad's shorts have gotten longer.

Page 108: Keep the Change No. 1 (A1): The 1 and the 0's have switched places. No. 2 (A3): Where did the coffee sign come from? No. 3 (B3 to C3): Her necklace has vanished. No. 4 (B4 to B5): The word CUPCAKE has appeared on the shelf. No. 5 (B4 to C4): The number of food containers has doubled. No. 6 (B5): Some mug has run off with the coffee. No. 7 (E3): You can never have too many chocolate chip cookies. No. 8 (E4): The cake plate has lost its pedestal.

Page 109: Funny Business No. 1 (A2 to A3): That view is enough to give you double vision. No. 2 (A4): That degree doesn't carry as much weight as it used to. No. 3 (B5): The finial on that lamp has a better vantage point now. No. 4 (C3): His hair has gotten slightly grayer. No. 5 (D2): That dude prefers the old-school quill and inkwell. Nos. 6 and 7 (D3): So, of course, he's ditched his pen. And a button on his jacket has fallen off. No. 8 (D4): The baseball has grown larger.

Page 110: Gone Fishin' No. 1 (A1): The seagull is nearing. No. 2 (A1 to A2): The orange light has been stretched out. No. 3 (A4): The flag's flap has flip-flopped. No. 4 (A5): One gull has cruised out of view. No. 5 (B1): And so has a boat. No. 6 (B2): Who opened the hatch? Nos. 7 and 8 (B3): That bird has turned to the right, and the trailer has vanished. No. 9 (B5): A few skids have been added to that pile. Nos. 10 and 11 (C1 to C2): The white stripe has been erased, and the boat is sinking. Nos. 12 and 13 (C2): That *D* is looking a bit droopy, and the windshield wiper has switched its position. No. 14 (C2 to D3): The skiff has been lengthened. No. 15 (C3): Did that post shrink? Nos. 16 and 17 (C4): A rope has been threaded through the freshly drilled hole. No. 18 (C4 to D5): Someone must have sprinkled some Patch Perfect along the dock. No. 19 (C5): The pile has grown taller. No. 20 (E4 to E5): A harbor seal has poked his head up for some air.

[GENIUS]

Page 114: Not a Creature Was Stirring . . . No. 1 (A2 to B1): The branches on the tree to the left have grown denser and longer. No. 2 (A2): The sickle moon is now full. No. 3 (A3): The spruce tree is facing the other way. No. 4 (B4): The wind must have blown off part of the television aerial. No. 5 (C1): The Christmas bush is getting taller. No. 6 (C2): One of the treetops along the horizon has been chopped down. No. 7 (C3 to D3): The top and bottom windows on the left side of the house have changed places. No. 8 (C4): Two of the attic windowpanes have been whitewashed. No. 9 (C4 to D4): One of the porch posts is gone. No. 10 (C4 to D5): Lights have been strung on that bush. No. 11 (C5): What happened to the drainpipe? No. 12 (D2): Someone has yanked the tank out of the snow. No. 13 (D3): The tree has moved precariously close to the house. Nos. 14 and 15 (D5): The garage door has narrowed, and the small patch of ground cover has vanished.

Page 116: The Old World No. 1 (A3): He's flipped over all the changes. Nos. 2 and 3 (A4): The candleholder is handle-less, and a slipper has lost its diagonal decoration. Nos. 4 and 5 (B1): The pen-and-ink set is minus one nib and a lid. No. 6 (B1 to C1): That cameo has gone from upright to head over heels. No. 7 (B2 to B3): Would the person who took Northumberland please put it back? No. 8 (B4): The ruby is now an emerald. Nos. 9 and 10 (B5): The brooch has replicated itself, and a stone has appeared in the left eye of the mask. No. 11 (C1): Be careful of the sealing ax—you might get cut. No. 12 (C3): The handle of the magnifying glass has been stretched out. No. 13 (C5 to D5): The gold locket doesn't have a chain to hang itself on. No. 14 (D1): The white ceramic disk is sliding down the map. Nos. 15 and 16 (D3): A shadow has been removed from that photo, and the black feather has turned crimson. No. 17 (E4): One of the stones on the hair clips has been stolen.

Page 118: Atta Buoy! No. 1 (A3): Where did that branch come from? No. 2 (B3): The reddish float has higher ambitions. No. 3 (C1): The white one has gained a stripe. No. 4 (C1 to C2): The net has been torn. No. 5 (C2): The leaf is covering up for the fence. No. 6 (C3 to C4): The black stripe has gotten fatter. Nos. 7 and 8 (C5): Someone has filed a 7 off the green buoy—maybe the same person moved the pole behind the net. No. 9 (D1): The crack in the green-and-red buoy has been repaired. No. 10 (D2): An *S* is missing. Nos. 11 and 12 (D3): The rope has been cut, and two knotholes have appeared on the plank. No. 13 (D4 to E4): Those boards have merged. No. 14 (D4): That float has flipped. No. 15 (D5): The rope is a bit longer. No. 16 (E1): Just what we need—another buoy. No. 17 (E3): That plant has sprouted up fast. No. 18 (E5): The pole has been snapped in two.

Page 120: Puppet Master No. 1 (A1): He seems even more downcast. No. 2 (A2): That guy has turned the other cheek. No. 3 (A3): The green man's scowl has become a smile. No. 4 (A4): The dot between his eyes has turned gray. No. 5 (A5): That dude could use some Visine. No. 6 (B2): His hand has disappeared. No. 7 (B3): He has rewrapped his scarf. No. 8 (B4): The purple puppet is scratching his chest. No. 9 (B5): Ol' Red Eye's belt has vanished. No. 10 (C1): Looks like somebody needs a haircut. No. 11 (C2 to D2): His pupils have been set farther apart. No. 12 (C2): The headdress has an extra pair of dots. No. 13 (C4 to E4): Her box has inched up. No. 14 (C4): And she's lost her hair ornament. No. 15 (C5 to E5): That box has straightened itself out. No. 16 (C5): The yellow ribbon has been clipped. No. 17 (D1 to E1): His decorative sash is gone. No. 18 (D3): That headdress has lost its flaps.

Page 121: Pony Up No. 1 (A1 to B1): That horse has lost his headgear. No. 2 (A3 to B2): A yellow pony has burst onto the scene. No. 3 (A3): What do they call a horse with two horns? A bicorn? No. 4 (B2 to C5): That equine has been

stretched out. No. 5 (B3): Another otter has joined the gang. No. 6 (B5): He's putting his foot down. No. 7 (C1): The workshop could use an extra mallet. No. 8 (C2): That horse has closed his mouth. Nos. 9, 10, and 11 (C3): The shelving brackets have gone missing, he's taken off his ring, and there's an additional spray can on the shelf. No. 12 (C4): Someone's been drilling holes in his hind leg. No. 13 (D4): That little fella has gotten a face-lift. No. 14 (D5 to E5): A box has vanished.

Page 122: Flower Power

10	8	16	5
3	13	2	15
6	1	12	14
11	4	7	9

Page 123: Feeling Lucky?

7	15	14	9
4	8	16	1
11	3	5	13
12	10	6	2

Page 124: Where the Heart Is No. 1 (A1): The shutter is taking over. No. 2 (A2): The lantern no longer has a hook. No. 3 (A3 to A4): The *A* is now a *V*. No. 4 (A4): She's taken the sign down. Nos. 5 and 6 (B2): Some slats have been added to the siding, and the door has lost its handle. Nos. 7 and 8 (B3): Her top has sprouted flowers, and the glass of milk has been filled. Nos. 9 and 10 (B5): A crescent has been carved into the shutter, and the window has been divided into thirds. Nos. 11 and 12 (C3): She's ditched her bracelet, and the lounger's been cropped. No. 13 (C4 to D5): The flowers have bloomed. No. 14 (C5 to E5): The garbage container is rolling away. No. 15 (D1): That urn is cracked. Nos. 16, 17, and 18 (D2): The board above the stairs has been smoothed out, that flowerpot is really living on the edge, and the belt of her robe has shrunk. No. 19 (D3 to E4): Another lantern has popped up. No. 20 (D3 to D4): The ledge under the pot has been extended. No. 21 (E1): One of the ladder's legs is missing. No. 22 (E1 to E2): Two stones have become one. No. 23 (E2 to E4): That step has been widened. No. 24 (E2 to E3): The pooch is sliding around. No. 25 (E4): One stone has been divided into two.

[ANIMALS]

Page 128: This Can't Be the Caribbean No. 1 (A5 to B5): A crane has stretched out of sight. No. 2 (B1 to C1): The ship is getting bigger. No. 3 (B2): And the stack has gotten taller. No. 4 (B4 to C3): The hull is turning bluer. No. 5 (C2 to C3): Extra portholes have been added. No. 6 (C4 to D4): The dancing penguins are now a trio. No. 7 (C5): A lonely little penguin has come into view. No. 8 (D1 to E1): That bird's been eating. No. 9 (D2 to E2): One of those penguins needed a little more breathing room. No. 10 (D3):

She's a real head-turner. No. 11 (D4): That guy is slipping away from the flock. No. 12 (D5): Another penguin has joined the party.

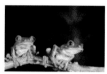

Page 130: **Come Here Often?** No. 1 (B3 to B5): Two more leaves have sprouted. No. 2 (C1 to C2): That frog's head has been enlarged. No. 3 (C1 to C4): They've traded eyes with each other. No. 4 (D2 to E2): The branch has cracked. No. 5 (D4): He's feeling awfully blue. No. 6 (E1): That toe is getting suspiciously longer. Nos. 7 and 8 (E3): One frog's toe is shrinking, while the other guy is twiddling his toes.

Page 131: **Quit Shoving!** No. 1 (B1 to B2): The stable's roof is expanding. No. 2 (B3): The lookout has gained height. No. 3 (B3 to C3): His shirt has turned blue. No. 4 (B4 to C4): Brownie's ahead by a nose. No. 5 (C1 to D1): An Appaloosa has sidestepped to the left. No. 6 (C1): The blue barrel has vamoosed. No. 7 (D1 to E1): That fence post is on its way up. No. 8 (D1 to E2): The white horse has moved left. No. 9 (D4 to E3): And his chocolaty twin has taken his old spot. No. 10 (D4): Someone's been messing with that diagonal bar. No. 11 (D5 to E5): He's first out of the gate.

Page 132: **Something's Fishy Here** No. 1 (A1 to A2): Quit clowning around. No. 2 (A2 to B3): Are the planes bothering you, Mr. Kong? No. 3 (A3 to D4): Lady Liberty is enjoying her new life among the reeds. No. 4 (A5): An angelfish has floated in. No. 5 (B1 to B2): One fish, two fish, I see a blue fish. No. 6 (B4 to B5): Shark! No. 7 (C3): A submarine has submerged into the fray. No. 8 (D1 to E1): Diver Dan, reporting for duty. No. 9 (D2 to E2): Someone's been noshing on these leaves. No. 10 (D5): That goldfish is golden. No. 11 (E1 to E2): Got butter? No. 12 (E2 to E3): There's the star of the tank. Nos. 13 and 14 (E5): A fish has emerged from those newly sprouted leaves.

Page 134: **Hello, Kitties** No. 1 (B4): Is that the same chair? No. 2 (B5): Curiosity might kill the rat. No. 3 (C2): At least the star is interested in the toys. No. 4 (C3): The kitten has scratched away part of the baseboard. No. 5 (D2): The cap and ball have been replaced by a feather. No. 6 (D3): That cat has gotten something off its chest. No. 7 (D4): The grass is ready for a trim. No. 8 (D5): The black-and-white cats now totally match. No. 9 (E2): The ball is bigger. No. 10 (E3): A catnip mouse has been tucked under that cat's paw. No. 11 (E3 to E4): The light blue patch of rug is slowly gaining ground. No. 12 (E4): Great—another toy they'll never touch.

Page 136: **Swanee, How I Love Ya!** No. 1 (B1): A swan has taken flight. Nos. 2 and 3 (B2): The boat is heading off, and it's now called the S.S. *LIFE*. No. 4 (B3): A few buoys have surfaced. No. 5 (B3 to B4): Call the *Weekly World News*—someone has parted the

land. No. 6 (B4 to C4): A bird has gone missing. No. 7 (B5): The captain has changed direction. No. 8 (C1): An extra swan has snuck in. No. 9 (C2): Who knew swans could stretch their necks so high? No. 10 (C4): That post is floating upward. No. 11 (D5): A swan is exiting stage right. No. 12 (E1): The piling has moved to a rather useless spot. No. 13 (E4 to E5): And more pilings are rising from the deep.

Page 138: **Dog Day Afternoon** No. 1 (A2): The portraits change often so no dog feels left out. No. 2 (A3 to A5): Apparently, the same goes for the abstract artwork. Nos. 3 and 4 (B4): The moon has set on Santa's sleigh, and there's a new kid in town. No. 5 (C2 to D3): The dog has switched spots with the pillow. No. 6 (C4): The fireplace is taller. No. 7 (D2): The lower middle square on the pillow has been rotated. No. 8 (D2 to D3): Dog biscuits, anyone? No. 9 (D3): A glass of wine for Fido. No. 10 (E4): The table may collapse.

Page 140: **See-through** No. 1 (A2 to B2): The butterfly's antenna has grown longer. No. 2 (A3 to B3): And two antennae have got to be better than one. No. 3 (C2 to C4): The forewings have swapped places. No. 4 (C3): The butterfly looks evil with those red eyes. No. 5 (C3 to E4): The hindwings have gotten a lot bigger. No. 6 (E2): A new scale has sprouted on its wing.

Page 141: **Move Along Now** No. 1 (A1 to A2): A longer log is all the better to trip the lions with. No. 2 (A2 to A3): He must have needed a new patch of grass to graze. No. 3 (A4 to A5): Yikes—who let her into this puzzle? No. 4 (B1 to C2): The doe has become a buck. No. 5 (C1): She's always sticking her nose in where it doesn't belong. No. 6 (C4 to D4): That gazelle has a lengthy neck and head. No. 7 (C5): And the other one has a huge noggin. No. 8 (D5): You can't hear without an ear.

Page 142: **Back of the Line** No. 1 (B4 to C5): The platform is tilting the other way. No. 2 (B5 to C5): That spire has grown taller. No. 3 (C1 to D1): He's turned his back on them. No. 4 (C3): His shirt has become green. Perhaps it's an indication of how he feels about the ride. No. 5 (D3): Show-off. No. 6 (D4): Swish that tail! No. 7 (D5 to E5): Whose trunk is that? No. 8 (E2): Don't trip on that rock.

[LIFE CLASSICS]

Page 146: **Heads A-Poppin'** No. 1 (A2): His third eye is showing. No. 2 (A3 to A4): Where did she come from? No. 3 (B2): His neck should hurt a lot less now. No. 4 (B3 to C3): Don't call her Four Eyes. No. 5 (B3): That guy's third eye has opened up wide. No. 6 (B4 to B5): She has taken a serious turn. No. 7 (B5 to C5): That girl is

ooking straight at you. No. 8 (C2 to D2): She's a mirror image now. No. 9 (D4): And she has a twin. No. 10 (E1): The droopy chap has got a doppelgänger, too. No. 11 (E3): Well, look who dropped in. No. 12 (E4): So there's where Four Eyes went.

Page 148: The Graduate No. 1 (A1 to B1): Her cap has swelled up. Nos. 2 and 3 (A4): The dog and the question mark have duplicated themselves, and their clones have migrated to that display. No. 4 (A4 to A5): That letter's split—must have been *T* time. No. 5 (B1): Her earring has doubled in size. No. 6 (B3): That is one confusing arrow. No. 7 (C2 to D2): Someone's closed the curtain. No. 8 (C3): Dial *M* for missing. No. 9 (D4): The giraffe has shifted to the right. No. 10 (E1): Her suit has become a dress. No. 11 (E3): The speaker has dropped down.

Page 150: Boob Tubes No. 1 (A1 to B1): The **V** in the middle of her sweater has been filled in. No. 2 (A3): That's a lot to ask for such a small TV. No. 3 (A4 to A5): It's, like, *Invasion of the Lamp Snatchers.* No. 4 (A4 to B5): That TV broadcasts tall tales. No. 5 (B1): Her sleeve is a little bit longer now. No. 6 (B2): The salesman has jacked up the price of that set. No. 7 (B3): The people on TV look familiar. No. 8 (B5): That large console is priced to steal. No. 9 (C4 to D5): Ah, the good old test pattern. Nos. 10 and 11 (E1 to E2): The ledge of the display window has dropped out, and knobs have been placed on the speakers. No. 12 (E3): That table could topple. No. 13 (E4): The speaker has been given another lightning bolt.

Page 151: Shakespeare Slept Here No. 1 (A3): The chimney has slipped down. No. 2 (A3 to A5): That roof is reaching its peak. No. 3 (B1 to B2): The apartment on the left is gonna need more Windex. No. 4 (C4 to D4): Someone's been playing with the molding. No. 5 (D1 to D2): Who took the beams? No. 6 (D3 to D4): The sign has widened. No. 7 (D4): It's plain that it's PLANE, not PLAIN. No. 8 (E1): A new sign o' the *Times* has appeared. No. 9 (E2): The blanket has lost a stripe.

Page 152: Life in the Burbs No. 1 (A1): The telephone pole is growing. No. 2 (A3 to A4): Don't laugh at that sign. No. 3 (A4): A zero has dropped out. No. 4 (B1): A new house has moved in. No. 5 (B3): A stack has vanished. No. 6 (C2 to E2): She's backing up. No. 7 (C3): His twin has popped in. No. 8 (C4 to E4): Junior's grabbing a better pole position. No. 9 (C5): The garage door is a little bit glassier. No. 10 (E3): The fire hydrant is turning circles.

Page 154: Haberdashery No. 1 (A1): Those hats are mew? No. 2 (B3): That light's in a new spot. No. 3 (C2): He's a growing boy, er, man. No. 4 (C3): His face is on the other side of the board. No. 5 (C3 to D3): His sleeve is longer. Nos. 6 and 7 (D3): The hammer has fallen, and the watch is gone. No. 8 (D3 to E3): The saw has been sawed off. No. 9 (D5): Who notched the lumber? Nos. 10 and 11 (E4): His foot and the board are bigger.

Page 156: Well Done No. 1 (A1 to A2): He's upgraded the range on the left. No. 2 (A3): The pipe is sliding back. No. 3 (A5): The chef's hat is a little smaller now. No. 4 (B3 to B4): The other range has shrunk. No. 5 (C3): The door has lost its mesh. No. 6 (E1): Yum—a second helping of, um, brown stuff. No. 7 (E5): The longer apron will keep his pants cleaner.

Page 158: Not Too Fast, Son No. 1 (A2 to B2): That can has shot up. No. 2 (A4 to A5): The rags are hanging on the right. No. 3 (B1 to B2): The hat has lost its band. No. 4 (B2 to C5): The scene beyond the windshield has been flipped. No. 5 (B4): A bigger mirror provides a better view. No. 6 (B5): The 1 and the 2 have switched places. No. 7 (C3): He has tucked his suspenders under his collar. No. 8 (C4): A tall handle is easier to grab. No. 9 (C5): Although, since the rod has broken off, the door may never open again. No. 10 (D1 to E2): Now that the box is bigger, maybe those guys can clear off the top shelf.

Page 160: Baggage Claim No. 1 (B1): The top of the dome has rotated. No. 2 (B1 to C1): A girl in a black skirt and a white blouse has wandered onto the plaza. Keep your eyes peeled—you'll see her again. No. 3 (B4 to C4): The man with the crossed arms has cloned himself and moved closer to the center of the action. No. 4 (C1): He's retracing his steps. Nos. 5 and 6 (C3): As promised, the lady appears for a second time . . . and once more. No. 7 (C3 to C4): With so many people around, this car better take it slow. No. 8 (C4): Someone's playing games with this sign. Nos. 9 and 10 (C5): The mother and child from the Burbs puzzle have returned, and that man taking in the scenery is new to the crowd. No. 11 (D1): Another suitcase has turned up. No. 12 (D3): The trunk is a little longer. Nos. 13 and 14 (D5): One of the suitcases has an extra sticker, but the other's a stranger to these parts.

New Guinness World Record:
Largest Spot the Difference Puzzle

Resistance Is Futile

The robots are coming, and they have flipped their gears.
Unless you can find all the changes, you will be assimilated.

80
changes

KEEP
SCORE

78min 15sec

Answers
on page 176

[CHAMPION]

Page 174: Resistance Is Futile

No. 1 (A1): What do you get when you mix a human and a robot? A cyborg.

No. 2 (A1): The 'borg has lost his upper arm.

No. 3 (A2): The blue button has turned green.

No. 4 (A2): Mrs. Potato Head has never looked more futuristic.

No. 5 (A2): What does an automaton need a mouth for, anyway?

No. 6 (A2): A hexagonal web has formed on his head.

No. 7 (A2): An eye has sprouted atop his noggin.

No. 8 (A2): You can't get far on a broken leg.

No. 9 (A2): The logo on the red 'bot has grown a tail.

No. 10 (A3): His shoulders have gone from green to blue.

No. 11 (A3): She's lost her middle cone.

No. 12 (A3): Where did that little robot come from?

No. 13 (A3): His green belt has become magenta.

No. 14 (A4): There's a PUZZLE on his torso.

No. 15 (A4): One of the feet in the background has vanished.

No. 16 (A4): The red-and-yellow fella looks surprised.

No. 17 (A4): And his gears have lost their colored centers.

No. 18 (A4): Dig that spiky hair!

No. 19 (A4): And it seems Spiky has drunk too much coffee.

No. 20 (A4): Plus, he likes to run rings around Saturn.

No. 21 (A4): Three eyes are better than two.

No. 22 (A4): The doohickey on Three Eye's head is getting redder.

No. 23 (A5): The yellow dot has a black center now.

No. 24 (A5): What happened to the red circle?

No. 25 (A5): And three little dots have multiplied into six.

No. 26 (A5): There's a loose gear rolling around.

No. 27 (A5): His leg has gained an extra stripe.

No. 28 (A5 to B5): Face flipping is a clever trick.

No. 29 (B1): All that's left of that guy is his head.

No. 30 (B1): Danger, Will Robinson!

No. 31 (B1): Two extra rows of dots have bloomed on his head.

No. 32 (B1): Is that how a robot winks?

No. 33 (B2 to B3): The silver automaton's pupils have turned yellow.

No. 34 (B3): And he got a nose job.

No. 35 (B3): An extra row of frills has been added to her apron.

No. 36 (B3 to C3): His hand has turned blue.

No. 37 (B4): Is that a rocket on his chest?

No. 38 (B4): The Statue of Liberty is making an appearance on his head. How patriotic.

No. 39 (B4): That guy seems happy.

No. 40 (B5): The green robot enjoys saying no.

No. 41 (B5): But the 'droid next to him says maybe.

No. 42 (B5): The squat, red fella has lost some dots.

No. 43 (B5): The power gauge has been rotated 90 degrees.

No. 44 (C1 to C2): *Eek*—a mouse is sniffing around down there.

No. 45 (C1): That automaton is showing a sign of LIFE.

No. 46 (C2): Can you PICTURE this?

No. 47 (C2): The bolt on his head has been beefed up—maybe it's a mating thing.

No. 48 (C2): A backward 7 still equals 7.

No. 49 (C2): The dot between his eyes has vanished.

No. 50 (C3): That's Mr. Robot to you.

No. 51 (C3): His claw has shrunk.

No. 52 (C3): That's a heckuva hole.

No. 53 (C3): *R.U.R.* stands for Rossum's Universal Robots.

No. 54 (C3 to C4): Hey—no racing in here!

No. 55 (C4): The silver clip on his chest has been cropped.

No. 56 (C4): And the rod on his leg has gotten longer.

No. 57 (C4): The sleepy cyborg's eyes are on the move.

No. 58 (C5): The littlest robot is hiding underfoot.

No. 59 (C5): Yet another bolt has grown.

No. 60 (C5 to D5): All the white dots have turned blue.

No. 61 (D1): The bolt-growing situation has officially become a pandemic.

No. 62 (D1): The colors on his chest panel have been changed.

No. 63 (D1 to D2): His headspring is now multicolored.

No. 64 (D2): The blue 'bot is a yes man for the new millennium.

No. 65 (D2): The rocket on the drum has been flipped over.

No. 66 (D2): Now he'll never be able to dance at the Metal Monsters' Ball.

No. 67 (D3): The drumstick has been trimmed.

No. 68 (D3): His death ray has doubled in size—just in time for the robot revolution.

No. 69 (D3 to E4): Everything about that tin man has been reversed.

No. 70 (D3): He also has a dial on his head.

No. 71 (D4): Sleepy's horizontal stripes have been enmeshed with the vertical ones.

No. 72 (D4 to D5): And a submarine is floating near him.

No. 73 (D5): The 3 and the 4 on that dial have exchanged places.

No. 74 (D5): The blue boy's foot has outgrown his leg.

No. 75 (D5): Did someone steal the gold pin from that robot's head?

No. 76 (E1): The white needle has swung to the right.

No. 77 (E1 to E2): Part of his foot has turned yellow.

No. 78 (E3): The red dots on his chest have gone green.

No. 79 (E5): The automaton's eyes have made a connection.

No. 80 (E5): The gauges indicate that his power has been restored.